**SIRSHREE**

# Journey to Enlightenment

Unfolding the Path to Ultimate Freedom

**Journey to Enlightenment**
By **Sirshree** Tejparkhi

Copyright © Tejgyan Global Foundation
All Rights Reserved 2022

Tejgyan Global Foundation is a charitable organization
with its headquarters in Pune, India.

ISBN : 978-93-90607-38-9

Published by WOW Publishings Pvt. Ltd., India

First edition published in February 2022

First reprint published in February 2025

Printed and bound by Trinity Academy, Pune, INDIA

This book is the translation of the Hindi book titled
"Moksh Path Rahasya" by Sirshree Tejparkhi.

Copyrights are reserved with Tejgyan Global Foundation and publishing rights are vested exclusively with WOW Publishings Pvt. Ltd. This book is sold subject to the condition that it shall not by way of trade or otherwise, be lent, resold, hired out, or otherwise circulated without the publisher's prior written consent in any form of binding or cover other than that in which it is published and without a similar condition including this condition being imposed on the subsequent purchaser and without limiting the rights under copyright reserved above, no part of this publication may be reproduced, stored in or introduced into a retrieval system, or transmitted, in any form, or by any means, electronic, mechanical, photocopying, recording or otherwise, without the prior written permission of both the copyright owner and the above-mentioned publisher of this book. Any person who does any unauthorized act in relation to this publication may be liable to criminal prosecution and civil claims for damages.

Although the author and publisher have made every effort to ensure accuracy of content in this book, they hereby disclaim any liability to any party for any loss, damage, or disruption caused by errors or omissions, resulting from negligence, accident, or any other cause. Readers are advised to take full responsibility to exercise discretion in understanding and applying the content of this book.

*To*
*King Harishchandra,*
*who is remembered even today,*
*for his truthfulness, generosity, and commitment;*
*who serves as an inspiration for seekers of Truth,*
*to keep their thirst for Truth alive*
*and walk the path to Enlightenment.*

# Contents

| | | |
|---|---|---|
| | Preface | 7 |
| **PART 1 - WHAT IS ENLIGHTENMENT** | | **11** |
| 1. | Enlightenment – The Vigilant Guard | 13 |
| 2. | Enlightenment is Nothing, and Nothing is Everything | 17 |
| 3. | The Path to Enlightenment – You Are a Traveler | 21 |
| 4. | Watching the Movie of Enlightenment | 24 |
| 5. | Why Enlightenment Doesn't Seem Worthwhile | 28 |
| 6. | Myths and Assumptions About Enlightenment | 34 |
| 7. | Extraordinary Path, Unparalleled Destination | 41 |
| **PART 2 - A BLEND OF UNDERSTANDING AND EXPERIENCE** | | **47** |
| 8. | The Origin of the World | 49 |
| 9. | Realizing One's True Nature | 53 |
| 10. | The Self's Mirror – The Body-Mind Mechanism | 58 |
| 11. | The Face of Enlightenment – Behind the Seven Masks | 64 |
| **PART 3 - ENLIGHTENMENT – TRUE FREEDOM** | | **69** |
| 12. | Understanding the Ego | 71 |
| 13. | The Trick To Avoid Getting Tricked by the Senses | 76 |
| 14. | Being Neutral to the Stress of the Senses | 81 |

| 15. | Overcoming the Delusion of Two Paths | 85 |
| 16. | Liberation From Multi-layered Existence | 92 |
| 17. | Getting Rid of Wrong Beliefs | 99 |
| 18. | The Garb of the Fake Personality | 108 |
| 19. | The Aggregation of Impressions and Tendencies | 115 |
| 20. | Letting Go of Insistence in Desiring | 121 |

| PART 4 - THE FIVE PILLARS OF ENLIGHTENMENT | | 127 |
|---|---|---|
| 21. | Pure Mind | 129 |
| 22. | Karma Without Bondage | 134 |
| 23. | Nectar of Devotion | 139 |
| 24. | Self-Introspection | 145 |
| 25. | Thirst and Grace | 150 |

## PREFACE
# Here and Now, Nowhere Else

*There is Happiness.*
*There is a reason for Happiness.*
*There is a way to attain Happiness.*
*There is a state of attainment of Happiness.*

These four great aphorisms point to that experience of ultimate bliss, which is the birthright of every human being. This bliss is beyond the polarities of joy and sorrow. It ceaselessly goes on since eternity and continues forever. It is untouched by situations, people, or conditions. It is boundless and everlasting, without a beginning or an end.

These great aphorisms are an auspicious news. They can eradicate the darkness of despair from the human mind by kindling the flame of hope. The experience of bliss is simple, straightforward, and indeed possible. Such an unending and limitless bliss does exist. There is a way to experience this bliss, which can be easily made possible through the human body.

Everyone seeks happiness alone but at the wrong place! Just as a musk deer seeks its own fragrance everywhere else but within itself, the human mind and senses seek fulfillment in worldly objects. Whatever we do—be it a job, business, art, study, or housework—the root cause behind our actions is the desire for happiness alone. However, as we are unaware of the ultimate bliss, we keep chasing fleeting happiness that diminishes with time. These momentary pleasures could be prosperity in the form of material comforts and conveniences, the happiness derived in relationships, or satisfaction drawn from name and fame.

Let us understand this with an example. Anand tops his class in the exams. Immediately, he rushes home and excitedly shows his performance card to his mother. Overjoyed, she happily hugs him and cooks his favorite sweet. The next day, he again shows her his performance card, "Mom, I topped my class!" She pats him, "Yes, dear! Very good." On the third day, he again tells his mother, "Mom, I topped my class!" While completing her chores, she replies, "Yes, I know!" When he repeats the same thing on the fourth day, his mother shouts at him, "I already know it. Why do you need to repeat it? Stop bugging me. I'll smack you if you tell me this one more time!"

Whoa! What happened here? She lovingly hugged him on the first day. Her joy knew no bounds. She distributed sweets to her neighbors and told them, "My son topped his class." And now…? Her happiness should have increased with time. She should have been happier after a week, a month, but this didn't happen. The joy of her son having topped the class ran its course in less than four to five days! Now it doesn't excite or gladden her. Instead, the same thing causes her anger after the initial joy wears off.

Everyone wants to be happy but live in the illusion that acquiring external objects will make them happy. So, they spend their life amassing things like property, expensive cars, acquiring academic qualifications, gaining positions in the organizational hierarchy, etc. They get deluded in the vain attempts to seek lasting happiness from others. They invest their life trying to make others happy, causing them tremendous stress.

We often mistake sensory pleasures for true happiness and indulge in delicious food, melodious music, captivating scenes, or delectable aromas. As we feed on sensory pleasures, it becomes a habit, and we find it hard to escape the trap of the illusory world. It provides better and better offers like going on a world tour, partying, showing off expensive mobiles, zipping around in the latest swanky car, etc., that seem to guarantee lasting happiness. But these pursuits fall short of delivering satisfaction and true happiness; the pleasure depreciates over time.

Take some time to introspect your life, how lasting or short-lived your experience of happiness has been, and how soon it vanished.

**True happiness does not fade with time; rather, it becomes brighter and augments with time.** Having experienced true happiness, you don't yearn for external pleasure; you feel contented all the time.

This permanent bliss is *Sat Chit Anand*—the bliss of existence that is conscious of itself. All the activities of the world are in the pursuit of this bliss. When this seeking attains fruition, it is called Enlightenment.

This book instills faith that this permanent bliss can be easily attained. It is possible to be free from the trap of limiting beliefs and tendencies and lead a life of boundless, eternal bliss. Believe in this book as a testimony of how interesting the beginning, middle phase, and destination of this inward journey can be.

**It is not necessary to wait for many lifetimes to experience Enlightenment. It is indeed available in this very lifetime—right here, right now, and nowhere else!**

The word Enlightenment has been considered synonymous with Self-realization, but there's a moot point that is underscored in this book.

Self-realization is the experience of the real 'I', the universal Self, which transcends all concepts, names and forms. It is the realization of our oneness with pure consciousness, through the direct experience of our true nature. The glory, beauty, simplicity, and immediacy of the state of Self-realization has been celebrated through hymns, poetry, discourses, and immense volumes of written work.

This book starts by discussing the essence of this experience and dispelling the myths around it. But it goes further and delves into the journey, the pitfalls you encounter, and the process of readying yourself for stabilizing in that state of Self-realization.

There are many who experience momentary flashes of oneness when they are with nature or even in the midst of their daily lives. However, these are only samples of the experience of Enlightenment which appear more pronounced when the understanding shines forth.

However, the journey should not stop with mere glimpses. The real purpose of life is to stabilize in the experience of Self-realization, to permanently abide in the experience of the Self and express its divine qualities of unconditional love, boundless bliss and peaceful stillness through the human body. That is Enlightenment!

Self-realization is incomplete, unless one attains Self-stabilization, followed by Self-expression. This book charts the journey that leads the seeker beyond mere glimpses of Self-realization to stabilize permanently in the sublime bliss of Enlightenment.

Without further ado, let's get started on this journey. Continue reading... here and now!

# PART 1

## WHAT IS ENLIGHTENMENT

With simple straightforward examples and analogies, this part of the book discusses Enlightenment in the context of everyday life. It also uncovers the prevalent beliefs about Enlightenment. In a nutshell, this part attempts to remove the veil of ignorance. So, let us now delve into this curtain-raiser.

# 1

# Enlightenment – The Vigilant Guard

*The Divine Truth is greater than any religion or creed or scripture or idea or philosophy.*

~ Sri Aurobindo

Enlightenment! Isn't it meant for those sages and saints who renounce the world and delve into deep sadhana and penance? We are householders who have to deal with the practical challenges of everyday living. We look after our families. We cannot abandon our households and families and go to the Himalayas to perform penance, like the hermits do.

Yet, we wish for liberation from negative thoughts, from the regrets of the past and anxiety of the future, from sorrow, stress, worry, and vices like boredom, depression, fear, guilt, and so on. These hindrances cloud the minds of those aspiring to lead a good life. They realize that they can lead a better life only after being liberated from all the negativities. They will be surprised to know that knowingly or unknowingly, their desire to be free is nothing but a prayer to attain Enlightenment!

The simple meaning of Enlightenment is complete liberation or total freedom. Various religions have given it different names viz. Nirvana, Kaivalya (a state of supreme solitude), or Param Padam (bliss at the lotus feet of the Lord). Whatever be the name, the important point is while the body is alive, we should attain liberation from things that degrade the quality of life, divert us from our true nature, prevent us from realizing our fullest potential, and entangle us in bondage. In other words, realizing our true nature is Enlightenment.

Once Sri Ramakrishna Paramahansa was asked by one of his disciples, "You meet the Goddess Mother Kali. You converse with her. Can you please send her to my place so that I can see her?" Sri Ramakrishna said, "Sure, I'll send her. Just give me your address." Overjoyed, the disciple gave his address and returned home. He felt that Mother Kali would visit him at his place.

Many days passed, but Mother Kali did not visit his house. The disciple returned to Sri Ramakrishna and asked, "Did you not send Mother Kali? She did not come to visit me." Sri Ramakrishna replied, "You gave the address of your house, but not yours. What is your address?" This time the disciple gave his office address. He could not grasp Sri Ramakrishna's hint. Sri Ramakrishna was actually asking for the address of the true Self, the real 'I'. He was trying to tell the disciple that he would be able to see God if he dwelled in his true nature. But the disciple could not decode his profound message and kept giving the address of his false 'I,' the body. But you would have understood the hint that to see God, we need to know who we truly are. Enlightenment has to do with realizing our true Self.

We get to know the true Self only after we know the false Self. The false address of the Self is the ego. When seen from a different perspective, Enlightenment is the liberation from birth and death of the ego. Let us understand this with an analogy.

A scientist experimented with the waves of an ocean. He placed a small blinking bulb on each wave, as he wanted to understand when the bulbs exactly switch on and off. He found that the bulbs remained switched off during any mundane talk. But when the waves were praised or accused, the bulbs switched on!

People from all over flocked to witness this experiment. They wanted to see how the bulbs turned on and off just by talking to the waves. When they praised the waves, "How beautiful the waves are! How high the waves are rising," the bulbs switched on. When they accused them, "Why are the waves rising so high? The water is so muddy," the bulbs switched on again! People were surprised to see this. Then they talked about mundane activities with the waves, "It's Monday today. I need to be at the office by 10 a.m. I'm going to have a bath now," the bulbs remained switched off.

Then a person approached the scientist and requested, "I want to speak to these waves in isolation where there is nobody else." The scientist made the necessary arrangement, and the person spoke to the waves in private.

After the person had spoken to the waves, the scientist noted a difference in the waves' behavior. Now the bulbs would not switch on, regardless of whatever they were told. Be it praise or accusation; the bulbs would remain switched off. The scientist was astonished; what exactly did that person tell the waves?!! When the person was asked, he told that he had shared the secret of Enlightenment with the waves, as a result of which the switching on and off of the bulbs had stopped permanently.

This analogy provides hints about the reality of human life. The waves represent human beings. The blinking bulbs on the waves represent the ego. As the ego rises, the bulb switches on. When the ego is dormant, the bulb switches off.

When some undesirable incidents cause sorrow, or someone blames you, the ego is hurt. You start thinking, "Why is this happening to me? How can the other person behave this way with me?" and the ego-bulb switches on! Similarly, when someone appreciates your work, your house, or your qualities, you consider this to be your success, and again, the ego-bulb lights up. Thus, the ego rises in both the situations—criticism and appreciation—and the bulb switches on.

If you want to do something but can't, anger arises due to the hurdle in fulfilling your desire. When people do not behave the way you want them to, you feel sad. If you visit your friend for a function and he doesn't welcome you warmly, you feel disappointed. In all such situations, the bulb switches on. When you are busy with mundane activities, your ego is dormant, and the bulb remains switched off. The rise and fall of the ego are incessantly happening in everyone. This is bondage, and the state that is attained when the birth and death of the ego permanently stops is Enlightenment.

When the Buddha attained Enlightenment, he exclaimed, "O Housebuilder (ego), now you are seen. You shall not build the house again." This means the Buddha realized how the individuality takes shape. He clearly saw what makes one assume oneself as an individual. He discovered how the ego rises and falls. Through direct experience, he understood exactly how and when one forgets one's true nature and lets the ego arise. Therefore, he could proclaim that the ego would never again be created.

The ego is the thief hidden within us. The moment we close our eyes in oblivion, the ego immediately springs into action. Only when the guard is vigilant can we know when the thief wakes up and gets into action. Enlightenment is the permanent vigilance of the guard within us!

# 2

# Enlightenment Is Nothing, and Nothing Is Everything

*When I look inside and see that I am nothing, that is wisdom.*
*When I look outside and see that I am everything, that is love.*
*And between these two, my life flows.*

~ Sri Nisargadatta Maharaj

There were many thorny bushes in a village. The roads were strewn with many thorns. While passing through the village, a traveler stepped on a thorn and started groaning in pain. The thorn had pierced quite deep in his sole. People from the neighborhood gathered around him and tried to help him get rid of the thorn. Someone gave him a needle to remove the thorn. Another villager brought some water to wash and clean the foot so that the thorn could be easily spotted. A third villager squeezed the foot so that the thorn could be weeded out.

Then a person came forward and put some drops in his eyes. The onlookers remarked, "What is he doing? Why is he putting medicine in his eyes when the problem is with his foot?" The person replied, "You're right. But since his eyesight is weak, I put medicine in his eyes to improve his eyesight. Due to weak eyesight, even after removing this thorn, he may step on another one and hurt himself.

Improved eyesight will enable him to remove the thorn himself. He won't need to suffer again."

Let us understand the deeper meaning behind this story. On the journey of Truth, there can be various thorns that prick a truth-seeker's mind. Despite making progress, he or she may still feel restless or dissatisfied and ponder, "Despite trying so hard, I've not yet been able to get rid of my tendencies. My mind is not at peace. When will I attain Enlightenment?"

There are a variety of techniques suggested in spirituality to alleviate suffering and attain mental solace. These techniques range from chanting, penance, wearing charms, and practicing rituals, to devotion, meditation, and practicing wisdom. If one understands the root cause of one's distress, one can figure out the truth on one's own and become free from all sorrows. The profound understanding of sorrow and happiness opens the eye of wisdom. This book expounds this profound understanding.

We all are quite familiar with the beliefs of heaven and hell. Many believe that heaven and hell are geographical places located somewhere beyond the earthly realm. However, the truth is that we all are carrying our own heaven or hell along with us, within us! We often feel like we are in hell on meeting certain people. These people tend to focus on deficiency, lack, and shortcomings in everyone. If we are not alert, their negativity infects our mind. On the other hand, we feel like we are in heaven on meeting some people. Such people always focus on the positive aspect of everything. We feel inspired by their company.

But Enlightenment is the third state that is beyond both heaven and hell. It is the state of nothingness. As hell is associated with negativity, nobody desires hell. The word heaven evokes a positive feeling. Happiness and abundance are associated with heaven. Hence, people aspire to live in heaven. However, Enlightenment does not appeal to people in the beginning. It seems useless and uninspiring as nothingness doesn't seem worthwhile! Everyone wishes to become something or the other. The truth is one can become something with some effort, but one must cease all effort and completely surrender to be nothing. Paradoxically, one has to do a lot to cease all effort! So, it doesn't seem easy to just be "nothing."

There was a wise saint who would always keep searching for something in the air. Once a person asked him, "What do you always keep searching for in the air?" The saint replied, "I'm searching for 'nothing'." The person asked, "And what will you gain after finding 'nothing'?" The saint smiled and replied, "Everything!"

We don't seek "nothing," and so we don't get "everything." This "nothing" is not the "no-thing" that the mind imagines or conceptualizes.

Our goal is to understand this "nothing." We have assumed many identities for ourselves in life, like, a doctor, an engineer, a Hindu, a Muslim, dark, fair, tall, short, smart, troubled, and so on. But these are mere labels attached to our body; we are not them. When we are rid of these labels, what remains is who-we-truly-are. It is nothingness, the state of Enlightenment.

Every night in deep sleep, the body, mind, and feelings disappear. We become free from actions, thoughts, and emotions. All the labels are removed, and we exist in the state of "nothing." As we dwell in the experience of nothingness during deep sleep, we feel cheerful and refreshed when we wake up in the morning. It's a different matter that emotions and thoughts engulf us as soon as we wake up, due to which that cheerfulness and freshness fade away. Enlightenment is experiencing this joy of nothingness even while we are awake. This is indeed possible. This book explains how.

To start with, while doing your everyday tasks, it helps to ask yourself, "Am I doing this work for the 'nothing' that I truly am, or for that 'something' that I am not?" For example, a person is watering plants in the garden. He sprinkles water on the flowers but leaves the stem and roots un-watered. What's going to happen? You may tell him, "Hey! You should water the plant at its roots." He may argue, "But there's nothing there – neither flowers nor leaves nor fruit. What's the point in watering there?" But that "nothing" is at the root of the plant! Unless he waters at the root, the plant won't flourish. That "nothing" is actually everything, and we all need to water it.

Contemplate: In your life, are you watering "nothing"? Or are you living life for something that you are not? Are you attempting to improve your inner understanding? Or are you engaged in amassing external laurels like social status, wealth, accomplishments, comforts, and so on? Let the thirst for Enlightenment remind you to water it. On watering Enlightenment, life will automatically blossom, open up, and creatively express itself.

Socrates was a wise saint. When he was sentenced to death, he was asked to carry out his own execution by consuming a deadly potion of the poisonous plant hemlock. While the death sentence was being carried out, his disciples asked him, "Where would you like to be buried after your death?" He replied, "You are indeed as ignorant as those poisoning me." His disciples were shocked. Socrates clarified, "They think they can poison me to death, and you think you can bury me. You are both fools because I am not who you assume. I can neither be killed nor buried. I am nothing."

Enlightenment is not a topic that can be explained in words, but words can point towards it. It is the wisdom of experiencing the Self. It can only be understood by being it. So, let's get ready to journey on the path to Enlightenment!

# 3

# The Path to Enlightenment – You Are a Traveler

*The soiled mirror never reflects the rays of the sun. Similarly, those who are impure in mind and heart can never perceive the grace and glory of God.*

~ Sri Ramakrishna Paramahansa

There is a story that dates to those times when man never used mirrors. In those times, there was a man who had a dream in which he vividly saw a face. He fell in love with it. Even after waking up, he could not forget that face.

He was restless and yearned to see that face again. Soon, he set out in search of that face. He looked around in every city and village nearby but could not locate that face.

In his quest, he reached a village near a mountain. He walked through the village enquiring about the face. The villagers told him, "We have never seen anyone that resembles your description. But there is a hermitage on top of the mountain. Go there and meet the Guru. If you are able to stay put and persevere there, you will surely find the face you seek." The villagers told him further, "Many people have visited this Guru before, but not all of them could persevere with him. Those who could persevere returned with immense bliss and fulfillment."

The person immediately climbed the mountain and met the Guru. He narrated the story of the face and expressed his desire to meet the person with the face. The Guru told him, "I'm willing to help you, but you will have to stay here, complete certain activities, and render service every day. Do you see those stones there? You will need to polish them to make some things from them." "I'm ready to do anything you say," the person happily agreed.

The Guru assigned him a stone to be polished. Every day, after completing his daily chores, he would sit and polish the stone. After a few days, he showed the stone to the Guru. The Guru advised him to polish it some more. He obeyed the Guru and continued polishing the stone. After tireless efforts over many months, he showed the stone to the Guru. Now, the stone had a shiny finish. However, the Guru was still not satisfied. He said, "This is not enough. It needs to be polished some more."

Many months passed by. The person kept polishing the stone. During these months, doubts started brewing in his mind, "What am I doing here? Have I come here to polish stones? Will I ever get to see that face again? This is becoming too much. I should give up everything and return home." But his thirst to see that face stopped him from leaving.

He would often ask the Guru, "After all, what's the use of polishing this stone? What's it got to do with the face I saw in my dream?" When he repeated this question a few times, the Guru warned him, "If you ask this question again, you'll be expelled from the hermitage." Seeing no other alternative, he kept polishing the stone.

The stone was so polished that it became smooth like a mirror one day. Suddenly the person could see his own face in that mirror. Seeing the face, he jumped in joy and exclaimed, "Wow! This is the very face that I've been searching for!" "I've found it! Finally, I've found it!" Cheerfully dancing on the way, he went to the Guru and said, "The face that I'd been searching for so many years... at last, I've found it in this stone!"

Smiling, the Guru revealed the secret, "This is no one else but your own self!"

There is a profound meaning behind this symbolic story. Our body has an external façade. But this story is about the inner essence.

Our inner essence is our real face; it is our true nature. The story symbolizes the journey where one falls in love with the real essence and embarks on a quest to realize it. This essence, in other words, has been called the supreme consciousness, the Self, God, Allah, Christ, or beingness.

Wandering from city to city, village to village, indicates seeking this essence outside. In the quest for the Truth, you may have seen that people visit places of worship and pilgrimage. They go on pilgrimages, attend spiritual discourses, read religious scriptures but do not attain the final Truth.

Finally, the seeker meets a complete Guru—one who is established in the experience of the Self. The seeker realizes the Self through direct experience in the presence of the Guru. Truth is not something to be known but rather experienced. When Self-realization happens through a body, the life lived through that body after that is supreme life.

Polishing the stone implies performing spiritual practice (sadhana), investing time in understanding the secrets of the inner world. Thirst for the Truth propels the seeker to practice sadhana. He honestly introspects his beliefs, preconceived notions, and assumptions and tries to identify and eliminate them. He witnesses the play of his ego in daily life. He reflects on the defilements and tendencies of his mind and tries to get rid of them. He keeps a vigilant eye on his response in every situation.

During this journey, the seeker can often get into the lull of complacency and feel that his sadhana is complete. He can thus stop without progressing further in the journey. But the complete Guru advises him, "Don't stop until you realize that inner face; persist until you are stabilized in your true nature."

The thirst for the Truth makes the seeker consistently practice sadhana. And truly, one day, he attains Enlightenment, where his body becomes a mirror for the Self. The Self witnesses itself through the medium of his body-mind. The Truth that was being desperately sought everywhere else was actually always already within him. Enlightenment is nothing else but simply knowing one's true nature.

# 4

# Watching the Movie of Enlightenment

*Know Thyself.*
*Self-knowledge is the supreme knowledge,*
*the knowledge of Truth.*

~ Sri Ramana Maharshi

A person has got a ticket to watch a movie at a multiplex cinema. Till he enters the multiplex, he is very clear about his objective. But on entering the multiplex, he watches the richly decorated shops there and begins window-shopping out of curiosity.

Then, various food counters grab his attention. You may have seen such food counters at cinemas where popcorn, sweet corn, soft drinks, beverages, and sandwiches are sold. His mouth starts watering, and soon, he explores them one by one. He has a pastry, then some popcorn, then some Belgian waffles, and then a pizza.

After satiating his craving, he looks around at the other stores where famous brands are on display. Clothes, shoes, wallets, and other accessories are on a buy-one-get-one-free offer. Their sight brings a twinkle in his eyes. He buys some clothes. Then he sees a photo studio there. He gets his pictures clicked in various poses.

He wonders, "Wow! This ticket is really useful. I could enter this multiplex and explore so many avenues of using it." Not even once does he remember, "Oh, what am I engrossed in? I've come here to watch a movie called, 'Enlightenment'!"

Such is the illusion of the multiplex world! We enter the multiplex with a ticket to watch the movie, but easily get captivated by distractions and forget to watch the movie itself!

After a while, this person realizes, "I've been roaming around for quite a while. Now I should go inside." At that very moment, someone in the crowd pushes him aside. He sees a tea stall in front and proceeds to get a cup of tea, but someone spills tea over him. He gets angry and yells, "Disgusting! Why do such things always happen with me?" Lost in these thoughts, he keeps wandering aimlessly. The thought of entering the theatre doesn't occur to him.

After a while, the show gets over, and people happily come out. He meets his acquaintance in the crowd, who tells him, "It would have been good if you too had made it inside." He laughs and says, "Yeah, I was going to." Eventually, the ticket expires, and he has to leave without watching the movie.

This analogy shows the carelessness and stupor that plague human life. Despite having a ticket in the form of a human body, man departs from the theatre of this world without watching the movie called "Enlightenment."

The multiplex cinema represents the material world, and the ticket is the human body. One can enter the multiplex to watch this movie only when one is born human. Enlightenment is possible only through the human body. No animal can get this experience as they lack the faculty of thinking; they don't possess the ability to understand the silent state within, and they lack the thirst for liberation.

Some other people may call the movie of "Enlightenment" by some other titles, like "True Happiness," "God," "Self-witnessing," or "Lord Almighty." Whatever be the name, the objective is to watch this film.

We generally tend to misuse the priceless ticket of human birth. We do everything else in life except meditate and abide in the Silence within. If at all we do sit for meditation, we don't exactly know what is to be done during meditation. So, we keep indulging in worldly thoughts even while our eyes are closed.

In the analogy, being lured by the various artifacts on display in the shops outside the theatre represents chasing the sensory desires of the material world. We are utterly and completely lost in enjoying delicious food, enchanting scenes, melodious music, fragrant aromas, and pleasing sensations. To gratify these desires, we need to earn money, so we get into the endless race of accumulating wealth and also get entangled in relationships. It has become almost impossible for us to free ourselves from these addictive attractions and get liberated.

The whole and sole purpose of human life is to realize our true nature and stabilize in it. This is true eternal happiness. But we get deluded into believing that our aim is to get educated, grow a career, get married, have children, raise, and educate them, get them married, and take care of grandchildren. We have believed that amassing material comforts and conveniences is true success. What an illusion! What an irony that we have time to roam around in the shops of the illusory world, but we don't have time to reflect on, "Why am I here on Earth?"

When people seem to have had enough joys from the worldly toys, some begin to feel dissatisfied despite having achieved worldly success. They feel a sense of emptiness deep within. A question arises in their mind, "Have I come on Earth just to accomplish all this? Isn't there any other purpose of being here?" A sense of dispassion from the material world arises within them, and they begin to feel that there is a missing link. This is an auspicious feeling. But out of ignorance, they feel it's something abnormal. To suppress this feeling, they indulge in sense gratification.

The illusory Maya never wants us to be free from its clutches. Today the temptations of Maya have increased manifold. It has become all the more easy to forget the real purpose of human life.

Often some people read or listen to Saint Kabir's *dohe*, Saint Meera's *bhajans*, the Dnyaneshwari, the Gita, the Quran, the Bible, or Saint Tukaram's *abhanga*. Some even attend discourses by spiritual gurus. But all this is done mechanically like a ritual. Some flock to spiritual congregations to satiate the hunger of their belly as there is food on offer. Some others throng to satisfy their intellectual curiosity. They are not prepared to practice the vigorous sadhana required to attain Enlightenment. This sadhana is symbolized as watching the movie of "Enlightenment."

Saint Tukaram, Saint Namdev, Jesus, Mohammed, Saint Kabir, and other self-realized souls entered this theatre and emerged enlightened. From that ultimate state of liberation, they asserted, "The whole and sole purpose of human birth is to know the inner world. Man's first goal is to make his mind unshakable and pure. Then, alone can he transcend his mind and stabilize in the state of nothingness. Actions performed while abiding in this state render him ultimate bliss and contentment."

Enlightenment is not limited to any specific person, community, race, or gender. It can blossom in any human being. Enlightenment is every human being's birthright because only human beings have the potential of attaining Enlightenment. Enlightenment is their primary goal. This is why it is said in the Vedic scriptures that even gods yearn for the human birth.

The ultimate purpose of the human body is to experience the Consciousness that transcends the body, mind, and intellect, the essence that enlivens the body. While living in the material world, we can make every incident a pretext for this experience. Leaving Earth without attaining this purpose is like skipping the movie despite having its ticket.

Let us not commit this mistake. Let us take full advantage of the ticket that we have received. Therefore, honestly contemplate: Am I merely engaged in gratifying the senses? Have I just accumulated knowledge without practicing it? Has an intense thirst for Enlightenment arisen within me? Have I set top priority for attaining the primary goal of being on Earth?

5

# Why Enlightenment Doesn't Seem Worthwhile

*There is no separate existence of God.
Everybody can attain Godhood by
making supreme efforts in the right direction.*

~ Lord Mahavir

You have made Enlightenment your goal and picked this book. Congratulations to you!

When one deviates from the purpose of life on Earth and follows other external pursuits, people congratulate him. Someone says, "I'm going to contest the elections; I seek political power." People congratulate him. Someone else says, "I want to contest for the Miss Universe title; I seek fame." People applaud her. Yet another says, "I want to win the World Cup; I seek glory." People cheer him. However, if someone says, "I seek Enlightenment," how many people would come forward to congratulate him? Nobody! Because Enlightenment doesn't seem worth pursuing, whereas seeking name, fame, status, position, prosperity, and power seem worthwhile. On the contrary, if someone wants to seek Enlightenment, his family, friends, and relatives try to pull him back.

Generally, people don't understand precisely what they will achieve on attaining Enlightenment. Usually, they understand the language of gain and loss. They are interested in seeking only such things that seem lucrative. Then why would they seek Enlightenment? What would they achieve on attaining Enlightenment? Neither name, nor fame, nor status, nor wealth! Nothing! That is why they do not make Enlightenment their goal. Well, at the very least, it is not their primary goal because they are not at all interested in "nothing." They do not know that the "nothing" experienced on Enlightenment is a state from which everything arises. Let us understand this with the help of an analogy.

A nightingale is imprisoned in a cage whose door is always open. Any wise person would advise the nightingale to escape from the cage.

Imagine yourself advising the nightingale, "The door of the cage is open. You can flee from the cage. Soar high in the sky and enjoy the freedom." The nightingale hears your advice and replies, "But this cage has this soft couch, a TV, and many gadgets. How can I leave all this behind? Where are such facilities in the open sky and the clouds outside? What if I fall out of the sky?" You become bewildered by the nightingale's logic.

The nightingale continues, "This cage is regularly cleaned. I get my food here on time. I share this cage with my partner. I like him very much. How can I leave him behind?"

When you tell her, "Why don't you take your partner along with you?" she replies, "No, he won't come with me. He likes it here." Here you may find the nightingale's arguments silly, but the truth is that we also make the same kind of excuses for not leaving our cages!

We all are imprisoned in our personal cages. There is a way to escape the cage, but most people wish to remain in the comfort-zone of the cage with all its conveniences to the extent that they are afraid of freedom. Let us understand why they are unable to make Enlightenment their goal with the help of this analogy.

1. **Priority is given to security and safety** – They get so used to the comforts of life that they do not want to give them up. They prioritize comforts over the goal. They are afraid of

leaving this sense of security to seek the unknown. They don't start the journey as they keep anticipating difficulties in such a journey.

2. **The cycle of desires** – In this worldly cage, whenever we eat delicious food, watch a beautiful scene, or hear a sweet melody, an impression is created on our senses. We feel enchanted by it. As soon as someone says, "Let's have a pizza today," an image of a pizza gets impressed in our eyes, and our mind starts craving it. Our nose remembers the smell and the tongue remembers the taste of the pizza. We start making plans to get a pizza in the evening and explore where to get it. This is just an example. If we apply it to any of our favorite things, we will feel the same. We feel restless until we acquire it.

   When images of such sights are impressed upon our eyes through advertisements, we no longer see the walls of the cage. And when those images disappear, the walls reappear. The fulfillment of desires creates a good feeling within us. Until this feeling persists, we don't sense the bondage of Maya. But as soon as its effect wears off, we sense a bad feeling, a feeling of incompleteness. The bondage of Maya begins to trouble us again. Then we start thinking of liberation from that feeling until we again get lost in the prison-attractions.

   The irony is that this desire for liberation lasts only for a short while until we again get lost in the attractions of the prison. Some other desire overpowers us soon, and we get entangled in pursuing it. The image of the new object impresses upon our eyes, the prison walls disappear, and the desire for liberation ends. Thus, this ceaseless cycle continues. Most people fall prey to such desires and are entrapped in bondage. Hence, they fail to persevere towards Enlightenment.

3. **Nobody reminds them of the loss of their original nature** – Usually, people speak about others' problems and difficulties. They say, "You don't seem to be healthy," "Your relatives are non-cooperative," "You're short of money," "You don't have your own house," "You lack talent," "You have no means to

earn a living," "Your boss is like this," "Your partner is like that," and so on. By repeatedly hearing such opinions, most people assume these as a cause of their sorrow. However, the root cause of all sorrow is our separation from our true nature. In the endless pursuit of desires, we lose our originality. However, we never grieve about having lost our originality. And no one reminds us, "I feel sorry that you have lost your originality. Sadly, you are lost to your own self." This is because people do not consider the loss of originality as a cause for sorrow.

4. **Escaping fears and sorrows** – Usually, most people prefer to escape instead of confronting their fears and sorrows. This tendency of escaping whatever seems unpleasant entangles them in bondage. To seek relief from the feeling of bondage, they get diverted into various distractions and addictions. Thinking about liberation becomes a remote possibility for them. Instead, if they muster the courage and patience to confront their inner truth, it can open the door to liberation.

5. **The web of old habits** – When a habit becomes ingrained within us, it becomes a tendency. With the onset of age, most people become a slave to their tendencies. Their tendencies grip them tightly and manipulate them in such a way that even at the time of death, they fail to realize this mistake. They prefer to dwell in the cage.

6. **Love for appreciation** – People appreciate those who excel in their field of activity. Hence, most people strive to reach the pinnacle of success in any field. Their ego is gratified when people hold them high. But no one applauds them for starting the journey towards liberation. In the famine of applause, they start feeling dull, as if the color has drained from their life. For this reason, they do not choose to walk the path to Enlightenment.

7. **The wishes of relatives** – In the story, the nightingale does not want to leave the cage because her partner does not want to leave the cage. She does not want to disappoint her partner.

Often, people do not want to leave their cage considering the wishes of their family members. They do not want to oppose their relatives. If Prince Siddhartha had thought, "If I relinquish my royal duties and proceed for penance to the forest, my parents will not like it, my family wouldn't like me taking the path to Enlightenment," then Lord Buddha would not have emerged.

8. **Emulating successful people** – Today, people assume that successful people speak after coming out of their cages. However, that is not the reality. They, too, speak from their cage. They, too, have similar weaknesses like others entrapped in bondage. When people become deluded that they can be successful by imitating these successful people, they don't feel attracted towards Enlightenment. They remain trapped in blind imitation of perceived success.

9. **First preference to family responsibilities** – Often, most people think, "Let me first get promoted. Let my children get married. Let me get settled first. Let me be financially sound first. Then I will devote myself fully towards the goal of Enlightenment." But as these responsibilities never end, the journey of Enlightenment never begins.

   At some point, they should realize, "If not now, then never," because worldly projects are bound to follow one after the other in life. They do not realize that if they prioritize Enlightenment, they will develop the required qualities for accomplishing their other projects more easily and effectively.

10. **Cage is the destiny** – Often, people mistake assuming this bondage to be natural. They are convinced that "Happiness and sorrow are both the bitter and sweet way of life." Hence, they cannot envision a state of equilibrium that transcends both happiness and sorrow.

Due to these reasons, most people are unable to make Enlightenment their goal. The illusory world pulls them. Saint Kabir has said, "Maya is the great enchantress, I know." Maya binds people in her attraction in such a way that they completely forget about

Enlightenment. Even if they make Enlightenment their goal, they are unable to make the effort to achieve it. Maya encroaches on them from various directions and deceives them in different ways. They can even be deceived for their entire life.

Hence, it is important to reflect on these reasons and strengthen the resolve for Enlightenment so that Maya doesn't deceive us.

Contemplate: What are the reasons hidden within you that prevent you from moving towards Enlightenment? What is your comfort zone or the conveniences that you are unable to give up?

# 6

# Myths and Assumptions About Enlightenment

*Happiness is your nature. It is not wrong to desire it. What is wrong is seeking it outside when it is inside.*

~ Sri Ramana Maharshi

In the previous chapter, we read how the nightingale does not want to escape from the cage despite the door to the cage being left open. She blabbers, "What will I gain by soaring high in the open sky? It will be difficult for me to fly in the open sky. It's meant for those who're already flying up there. I may fall even before I soar. I have my whole life ahead of me to enjoy all these comforts. I can fly later. I will think about it after fifty years," and so on.

From the nightingale's words, you can clearly see that her firm belief about liberation is untrue. The same thing happens with most people as well. They have also formed many myths about Enlightenment. Myths are wrong assumptions and opinions that the mind believes to be true. It is like the mirage in the desert – an illusion. It appears to be true, but actually it isn't.

Many myths related to Enlightenment have made their home in most minds due to which people hesitate to embark on this journey.

Even if they do start, they are always in a dilemma. Let us explore these myths to become free from them and progress on the journey without any doubt or dilemma.

1. **Myth** – Enlightenment can be attained only after death.

   **Revelation** – The state of Enlightenment is available in this life, here and now.

One of the most prevalent myths about Enlightenment is that one who does virtuous deeds on Earth will attain Enlightenment after death. In other words, one gets liberated from the cycle of birth and death thereafter. Nothing can be farther from the truth. It will not be an exaggeration if this myth is called the greatest irony of spirituality. This myth has closed the door to Enlightenment because most people do not find it motivating to achieve something after death. Enlightenment is a life filled with boundless bliss, where actions arise from perfect wisdom. Such a life is indeed lived here on Earth after becoming free from the bondage of Maya. It is the tranquil state that every human being prays for or calls out to experience in moments of sorrow. The moment he becomes free from his deepest myths is the moment of Enlightenment.

2. **Myth** – Enlightenment is about gaining a lot of spiritual knowledge.

   **Revelation** – Enlightenment is experiencing the knowledge of who-we-truly-are.

Let us understand this with a story. A saint used to visit a temple on the hill every day to see deity. There were many beautifully sculpted pillars outside the temple inscribed with spiritual messages and mythological stories. Every day the saint would go to the temple and read messages inscribed on one of the pillars.

The first day, he read about the principle of karma and destiny and stories about how someone performed karma and begot its fruit. That day, he learned the knowledge of karma and its fruit.

The second day, the pillar that he read from had pictures of heaven and hell. He learned about life in hell and heaven, what kind of people go where, etc.

Thus, he would go to the temple every day, read these messages inscribed on each pillar outside the temple, and return. Having gained the knowledge inscribed on the beautiful pillars outside, he believed that his journey towards Enlightenment was progressing well. Surprisingly, he never thought of entering the temple to see the deity inside. He gained knowledge about the deity but never even once saw the deity himself. In other words, he gathered bookish knowledge but never got first-hand experience of the Self.

Most people make this mistake in their journey towards Enlightenment. They gather spiritual knowledge by reading a plethora of books and start believing that they have understood everything. But all the knowledge remains merely in theory as they don't realize it through direct experience. It is akin to understanding everything about the sweetness of jaggery but never tasting it.

The objective behind gaining knowledge should be to understand it intellectually first and then realize it at the experiential level. A seeker can experience freedom from the bondage of Maya only on attaining the experience of the Self.

3. **Myth** – One should seek Enlightenment only after one's productive phase of life.

   **Revelation** – One should strive to attain the knowledge of the Self at the earliest.

While leading life on Earth, the sooner one gains the knowledge of the Self and assimilates it, the better. One then gets the opportunity to lead the remaining part of his life with peak awareness and clarity. In fact, attaining Enlightenment is not only the ultimate goal of life, but also the prerequisite for expressing one's fullest potential. Therefore, the earlier one attains Enlightenment, the better one gets the opportunity to express it.

You would have heard about the lives of many great masters like Saint Dnyaneshwar, Swami Vivekananda, Ramana Maharshi, Prince Siddhartha. They started their inner journey at a very young age, attained Enlightenment, and then spent the remainder of their life in the expression of the Self. Common sense also says that leading life in oblivion leads to many mistakes causing more karmic bondage. Instead, the earlier one starts living in awareness with wisdom, the better is his possibility of leading a blissful life.

4. **Myth** – One needs to perform rigorous penance and arduous spiritual practices to attain Enlightenment.

   **Revelation** – It is easier to attain Enlightenment with the path of understanding.

Some gurus preach with certainty that rigorous penance is required to attain Enlightenment. They impress upon their disciples that they should practice yoga, meditation, and several other spiritual practices most of the time every day. Disciples are enjoined to undertake arduous fast and chanting, perform penance, study voluminous literature on spirituality.

The truth is that a few moments spent in meditation regularly with the right understanding can help us dwell in the state of pure awareness for the whole day. It is always good to meditate for a longer time. It helps the body-mind become more disciplined and focused. It augments willpower. But it won't surely lead to Enlightenment. Meditation with the right understanding is more important.

There is a school of thought that professes that one can attain Enlightenment only on awakening the power of the *Kundalini*, which is experienced like the brilliance of a thousand suns. Some others consider the attainment of supernatural powers as Enlightenment. The awakening of the Kundalini and being endowed with spiritual powers is an experience associated with the body. In contrast, Enlightenment is an experience beyond the body and the mind.

5. **Myth** – Enlightenment is possible only for sages and saints, not for householders. One needs to renounce the material world to attain Enlightenment.

   **Revelation** – One need not leave the material world to attain Enlightenment.

There was a time when renouncing the world was recommended as the standard practice for attaining Self-knowledge. In different eras, as per the needs of those times, various saints founded different traditions. Some emphasized renunciation to attain Self-knowledge, while others had no concerns with being lay householders. No path is wrong. The understanding that backs our thoughts and actions is more important.

Today, you neither need to become a renunciate nor a householder, but rather a bright householder. A bright householder lives in the world fulfilling his responsibilities, like a blooming lotus in the swamp. A lotus blooms in the swamp but remains above the mud – completely detached from it, unblemished by the dirt. In the same way, one should attain the understanding of being detached from Maya while dwelling in it. This will lead to Enlightenment.

King Janaka, Guru Nanak, Saint Kabir, Saint Tukaram attained Enlightenment while discharging their worldly duties.

6. **Myth** – Attainment of Enlightenment and worldly pursuits are two opposing paths.

    **Revelation** – When one pursues the ultimate goal of life, his worldly goals get accomplished as a bonus.

This myth is more prevalent among the youth. They feel that spending time in spiritual pursuit can only come at the cost of achieving their worldly goals. They have so much to achieve - grow a career, develop skills and expertise, acquire a good house, get married, tour the world, and so on. If they pursue Enlightenment, how can they accomplish all these worldly pursuits?

Just think, if you aim to build a good house, will you separately worry about building a bedroom? No, because while the house is built, the bedroom will also be built as a part of it. The goal of Enlightenment is just like that. It is the complete and fundamental goal that progresses all other goals.

7. **Myth** – Enlightenment is seeing the deity's image mentally conceived as God.

    **Revelation** – Enlightenment is realizing the experience of the Self beyond the mind and senses.

Some people conceive God in an idol. They believe that getting to see God as depicted by the idol is Enlightenment. For example, some wish to see Lord Krishna, others Lord Rama and yet others wish to see the kind-hearted Lord Shiva, either in a dream or through other means. They seek Enlightenment in such externalized visions, whereas it is actually an inner journey.

8. **Myth** – Enlightenment is a rare occurrence; only a few can attain it.

    **Revelation** – Every human being holds the possibility of attaining Enlightenment.

Nature doesn't play favorites. It has bestowed the possibility of blooming to the fullest in every human being without any discrimination. The very purpose of human birth is to attain Enlightenment. The myth that only a few can attain Enlightenment has taken root in people's minds because they have heard the names of only a few enlightened masters. The songs of devotion, poems, teachings of these masters made them more renowned in the masses.

Many other great masters also attained Enlightenment and went into a state of quietude thereafter. No separate individual existed there who claimed to have attained Enlightenment. Hence, they were not known to the masses.

Do you know who all were there in the company of Lord Buddha or Lord Mahavir, who attained Self-realization? Have you ever tried to know their names? Many disciples of Ramana Maharshi were Self-realized. But very few became famous. As their names were never published, no one knew about them.

The Self expressed Itself through many bodies in the form of silence. They neither delivered any discourses, nor sang songs of devotion, nor composed poems. They just remained in silence. Nobody knows about them either. Some of them became famous because people encountered them by chance and wrote books about them.

You would have understood by now how baseless this myth about Enlightenment is. **The world has never been devoid of Self-realized souls. Self-realized souls have been playing a pivotal**

**role in the functioning of the world – some through interaction, while others through their mere presence in silence.**

Contemplate whether you still hold such myths:

- Enlightenment is attained only after death.
- One should bother about Enlightenment only after one has crossed one's productive phase of life.
- Enlightenment is rare.
- Only saints and ascetics can attain it.

7

# Extraordinary Path, Unparalleled Destination

*There are only two mistakes one can make on the path to Truth –
Not starting, and not going all the way.*

~ The Buddha

Consider, you are planning to visit a hill station, like Mahabaleshwar (a town famous as a holiday spot nestled in the hills of the Deccan plateau in Western India). As you have heard a lot about its beauty, you are engrossed in imagining the pleasure you will experience on reaching there. "It will be great fun to be drenched in the rain there. We will walk amid the clouds that blanket the hills! How enchanting the waterfalls will be! I look forward to visit the Sunset point and the Echo point in those hills!" You're excited and eager to be there.

As you start your journey, your car slowly winds its way through the hilly terrain. You are awestruck by the captivating vistas and overwhelmed with joy. Though you haven't yet reached the destination (Mahabaleshwar), the breathtaking scenes and pleasant weather fill you with so much joy that your eagerness and excitement about what you will do on reaching the destination ceases. Now you're totally in the present, enjoying the journey. Your journey, in itself, has become a source of happiness!

The journey to Enlightenment is also similar. You experience the "WOW!" effect not only when you reach the destination, but also during the journey. It is a unique journey because of various aspects. Let's understand these aspects.

1. **Extraordinary path, Unparalleled destination**

   The destination of this journey is unparalleled because it is the ultimate goal of human life, on the attainment of which no other goal remains to be achieved. The path leading to this goal is extraordinary. Even before one reaches the destination, one gets to experience true bliss even during the spiritual journey.

   When a seeker starts his inner journey, he listens to discourses, studies literature on the Truth, and practices meditation. He begins to experience a newfound peace. Gradually, he also begins to experience freedom from his behavioral patterns, false beliefs, and tendencies. He begins to break free from the clutches of Maya. These small victories that appear as milestones on the path give joy. This joy of liberation that he experiences propels him even deeper on this inward journey. This is the uniqueness of the journey to Enlightenment – not only is the destination beautiful, but the path is also filled with happiness and progress.

2. **A profitable deal**

   When one achieves success in all endeavors, it is said, "His bread is buttered on both sides." And so is the decision to walk the path of Enlightenment. Let us understand how.

   Three friends lived in a village. All of them suffered from an incurable disease. Some village elders advised them to visit a temple in the nearby kingdom. This temple was atop a mountain that was very difficult to climb. Whoever could make it to the temple and witness the deity were cured of their illnesses. As they all wanted to be cured, they decided to visit the temple to seek the deity.

As they found climbing up the mountain cumbersome, the journey to the temple seemed troublesome. The first friend panicked and felt discouraged about embarking on this arduous journey. He decided not to climb further to the temple. He explained, "It is better to bear the pain of the disease than to go through the pain of such a treacherous climb." The remaining two friends continued climbing. They wanted to reach the temple at any cost as they valued and loved their health.

One of them happily accepted the difficulties they encountered along the way because his focus was on seeing the deity rather than the difficulties. To his surprise, as he continued climbing higher, it became smoother and easier. After some time, he could enter the temple and see the deity. He could get cured of his illness and gain complete health.

The third friend was also making progress. He, too, loved being healthy. His attention got distracted by the various paths that led to the temple. He kept changing his path up the mountain. From time to time, he doubted, "Will I ever reach the temple this way?" Yet, he kept trying. He strained himself beyond his physical capacity. But just as he reached the temple, he got so exhausted that his life story ended before he could enter the temple.

In this example, the deity of the temple symbolizes Enlightenment. The three friends are novice seekers who want to safeguard themselves from the disease of Maya and gain the health of Truth.

Let us understand what happened to the first friend. Presuming that attaining Enlightenment was tough, he did not even begin the journey. He also prioritized comforts over the goal of life. By abandoning his journey, he aggravated his suffering. In other words, his desires and tendencies began to run amok. He lived a life of bondage by being limited to his comfort zone. As a result, he could not experience true happiness and contentment either here on Earth or hereafter.

What happened to the third friend who could not make it inside the temple? Some people perform spiritual practices all their lives, but they remain stuck in their tendencies due to a lack of conviction and proper guidance. Whatever be the reason, such seekers do get a glimpse of Self-realization but are unable to stabilize in that experience. They leave their bodies before that. Still, they benefit from the journey as they become free from their defilements and purify their mind during the journey. They also perform selfless deeds for the wellbeing of humanity and develop many good qualities within them. By increasing their understanding through a regular practice of sadhana, they are freed from the clutches of Maya to a great extent. This helps improve their condition both in this life and the afterlife. They spend their life on Earth happily and express at higher levels of consciousness.

The second friend was able to reach the temple and see the deity. In other words, he could realize the experience of the Self and prepare to lead life by abiding in the Self. On the spiritual path, when a seeker is able to follow the guidelines of an enlightened master and introspect honestly, his resistance and ignorance get eradicated. With faith, he focuses his attention in the right direction and attains his goal.

It becomes clear from the story that one shoots oneself in the foot by denying the path of spirituality. In contrast, it is a wise decision to undertake the inner journey. It is beneficial in all situations.

In the Bhagavad Gita, when Arjuna asked Lord Krishna, "O Madhusudana, what happens to those people who walk the path of Yoga but are unable to attain God? On the path of attaining God, do the deluded and shelter-less people get stranded on both sides and perish?"

Seekers like Arjuna first assume that they can experience supreme bliss only after attaining Enlightenment. Hence, they also experience fear, "What will happen if I do not attain Enlightenment? Will my spiritual practice be in vain? I will neither enjoy Maya nor attain God."

To eliminate these doubts from Arjuna's mind, Lord Krishna explained, "O Partha, there is no downfall for those who strive towards their inner growth or Enlightenment. They take birth in an illustrious family of wise Yogis, which becomes conducive for their further growth. Thus, any effort undertaken towards the goal of Enlightenment is never in vain."

3. **A natural journey**

The journey of Enlightenment is also unique because it is natural. You may be surprised to learn that every person is naturally driven towards spiritual progress. Common sense also suggests that if life itself naturally leads us towards Enlightenment, achieving this goal should be quite simple. But due to ignorance and lack of the right assessment, we fail to understand it.

We can automatically progress towards Enlightenment by tiding through life's challenges smoothly without resisting them. But most people complain or get attached to their desires. They declare, "Something wrong is happening," and resist whatever is happening. The moment they sense a sorrowful feeling, they feel something wrong is happening to them. Instead, if we watch this feeling with awareness, we will realize that the feeling has come to awaken us. People believe that they have to do something to be enlightened. The truth is that we do not need to do anything specific but just remain detached and observe how incidents unfolding in our life are naturally leading us towards spiritual progress.

In everyday life, we come across many opportunities where we can become aware and respond to situations by abiding in our true nature. In fact, we should make all incidents instrumental for our spiritual progress. For example, King Harishchandra encountered many trials in his life, but he faced them gracefully with truthfulness. He converted them into stepping-stones for spiritual progress. By being aware, he responded to situations intuitively. This practice led him to Enlightenment.

We can progress on this journey while fulfilling our worldly duties like Saint Kabir did while weaving yarn and Saint Ravidas while stitching shoes. The truth is that the entire universe is striving to lead us towards Enlightenment, provided we understand it.

4.  **Enlightenment here and now**

    The journey of Enlightenment is unique because its destination is available "here and now." Hence, there is no question of going anywhere outside but seeking within. There is a process of being stabilized in the Self.

    Let us understand this with the example of butter. Butter is extracted from milk, but we cannot see butter anywhere in milk. We can extract butter from milk only by following the process of churning. Similarly, Enlightenment is the state of stabilizing in the experience of the Self. This state is already always available inherently within us and can be extracted only by the churning practice of sadhana!

# PART 2

# A BLEND OF UNDERSTANDING AND EXPERIENCE

In the previous part, we looked at what Enlightenment is and how it is the ultimate goal of human life. Now we will understand what the state of Enlightenment is and how to experience it.

Often, a seeker knows about the state of Enlightenment in words. But it is to be directly experienced; mere words are not enough. Most people have heard that, "God resides within everyone," but that does not change their life. Life changes only after experiencing it. When knowledge is lived at the level of experience, it begins to transform life.

The forthcoming chapters will synergize knowledge and experience.

# 8

# The Origin of the World

*Thou hast a thousand eyes and yet not one eye;*
*Thou hast a thousand forms and yet not one form.*

~ Guru Nanak

When you decide to go on vacation to a tourist destination, you first gather information about it. How far is it from your city? How long does it take to reach? How is the weather there? How are the hotels there? Where can you get the food, you like? What are the must-see attractions there? You gather the minutest details about the place and then start your journey.

Imagine, if you can prepare so much for a short vacation, how much you would need to prepare for the journey to Enlightenment! In this journey, you need to understand, "What is this world, this cosmos? Who am I? What is the relationship between the world and me? What is Self-realization? How can I dwell in that state all the time?" Let us understand this with an analogy.

There was a solitary banana tree in a forest with only one leaf. There was nothing else in the entire forest other than this tree. Early morning, a dewdrop fell on the solitary leaf of this tree. Then, slowly, many more dewdrops gathered on the leaf. At sunrise, the rays of the sun fell upon the dewdrops, and every drop started reflecting the sunlight. The sun started radiating through every drop. As soon as the sunlight fell on the dewdrops, slowly, they started moving on the surface of the leaf. They started drifting in all directions, forward, backward, left, and right.

The dewdrops were still moving, and suddenly a storm broke loose. Clouds of dirt and dust started rising due to the gusts of wind. The dirt got mixed with some dewdrops, and the scene changed. Now, the leaf had some muddy dewdrops besides some transparent ones. Although sunlight was falling on all the drops, it reflected only through the transparent drops. When the sunlight passed through the dewdrops, a rainbow was formed. The seven colors of the rainbow blended to produce many more colors, forming a bouquet of vivid colors.

In the analogy, the dewdrop symbolizes a human being, while the sun is the Universal consciousness, the Self, the Source. The storm represents incidents happening in human life, and the dirt-dust signifies negativity. The seven colors of the rainbow together creating a bouquet of colors signifies how people come together to create a family, families create a community, communities create a nation, nations make up the world, and worlds make up the universe. In short, the universe is created by one manifesting as many. The analogy also explains that there is one sun, but its reflection shines within every dewdrop. Water exists as dewdrops as well as the vapor that is blown around in the wind. In the same way, the fundamental essence – the Self – from which the universe is created also exists within everyone.

However, when one gets influenced by Maya, one remains bereft of this experience of oneness and regards oneself separate from others. One identifies with the body, due to which one gets defined by the body's appearance, name, community, profession, etc. As a result, one considers other bodies to be separate from oneself. Slowly, the feeling of "I, me, mine," "you, yours" gets ingrained. Under the influence of Maya, one completely forgets the Self that pervades every being and starts behaving based on this ignorance. As a result, the dust of negativity impregnates the mind. The experience of the Self gets clouded just like the reflection of sunlight in the dewdrop is dulled by the dust and dirt.

Only after this dust of ignorance gets cleared does the Self begin to shine forth through the body again. Then one experiences oneness with every living being.

But the layman fails to understand how the same experience can exist within each one. What is this all-encompassing experience that exists within and outside everyone? Let us understand this experience with the help of an analogy.

In the rainy season, puddles of rainwater are formed on earth. The moon gets reflected in all the puddles. It is as if there are several moons. But the real moon is only one. The same moon shines through each puddle. Each puddle only serves to reflect the same moon.

In the same way, the same Self is peeping through your body-mind as well as that of others. You are a miniature replica of the universe. Considering the vast expanse of the infinite Self outside, it is very difficult to know it outside. A common man does not have the capacity to comprehend it all at once. It is but obvious to experience it within yourself first. If you realize it within your own body-mind, you can realize it outside within every other being too.

When Lord Krishna revealed his cosmic form to Arjuna on the battlefield of Kurukshetra, Arjuna was awestruck and overwhelmed at the same time. He pleaded, "O Lord, I am not worthy of beholding your grand form. Please revert to your subtle form." Lord Krishna then instructed Arjuna to seek the same experience within himself.

Hence it is better to direct our journey inward. If we realize the Self within, we will be able to realize it outside as well. It is just like the sweet rasgulla that is soaked in sugar syrup within as well as immersed in it outside. If the rasgulla is able to taste the syrup within itself, it will automatically know the taste of the syrup outside as well.

The Self alone pervades the entire universe. You may call it the Source, God, Almighty, and so on. Whatever be the name, everything has originated from it. The goal of human life is to realize it through our own experience and lead life by abiding in it. This is the attainment of Enlightenment while being alive in the human body-mind.

The experience of the Self is realized in meditation using the medium of the body. The body is made up of five elements viz. earth, fire, water, air, and ether, and five senses viz. eyes, ears, nose, skin, and tongue. It is not just any ordinary machine, but it serves as a mirror for the Self to experience Itself. The mirror is limited and small, so the limitless Self also mistakes Itself to be small and limited like the human body. However, whatever is visible in the mirror is but a small sample of the infinite. We must reach the ultimate by holding onto this thread.

Whether the body exists or not, the experience of Self is always present. However, experiencing the Self without the body is just as impossible as making steam without water. The body-mind is an instrument, the only means of attaining Enlightenment. It is the form through which the formless can be experienced. This is why the human body has been praised so much. This is why so much emphasis has been given to make the body a temple so that the Self can be experienced through it. A clean, pure, and healthy body-mind can function as a mirror effectively. Otherwise, if there are blemishes and stains on the mirror, the reflection also seems clouded.

## 9

# Realizing One's True Nature

*He who has overcome his fears will truly be free.*

~ Aristotle

In the last chapter, we learned that the body-mind serves as a mirror for the experience of the Self. However, under the influence of Maya, the Self forgets its true nature and identifies with the body. This fundamental mistake puts the very purpose of the human body-mind at stake. The limitless all-pervading Self lives the fragmented and divided life of an individual.

The first division is external, where the Self considers itself separate from others and gets stuck in "I, me, mine, you, yours." It fails to recognize its all-pervading essence within everyone.

The second division is internal, where the Self keeps associating with changing identities. Sometimes it identifies with the body, sometimes with the mind, and at other times with the intellect. It gets so involved in the stories of the body and mind that the thought about transcending them and dwelling in its original state of beingness never occurs to the Self. It spends the entire life of the body-mind assuming Itself as a limited individual.

The primary goal of human life is to break free of this divided life, know and dwell in our true nature. To put an end to this fragmented way of life, persistently ask yourself, "Who am I?" This question will lead you to the point from where the division began. It will take you to your core and unite with your true nature.

When you ask yourself, "Who am I?" many answers will emerge. For example, "I am <<*your name*>>. I am a Hindu. I am a Muslim. I am a man. I am a woman. I am a father. I am a boss. I am a student. I am dark. I am fair. I am intelligent. I am an idiot. I am a businessman. I am a doctor. I am a teacher. I am a landlord. I am a tenant," and so on. If you reflect on these answers, you will realize the assumption, "I am the body," at the root of them all. You give these answers assuming yourself to be the body because that is what you have heard about yourself ever since your childhood.

When you conduct an honest self-inquiry regularly, you will realize that when you say, "I went to the market" or "I went to the office," you assume yourself to be the body. When you say, "I thought of this idea" or "I solved this puzzle," you assume yourself to be the intellect. When you say, "I am sad," you assume yourself to be the mind. In this way, sometimes you consider yourself the body, the mind, or the intellect. Every time, your point of reference (center) keeps changing. This is the fundamental mistake.

The distance from any point on a circle to its center is the same. All the radial lines drawn from the circle to its center tally. However, if the center of the circle were to be shifted slightly to one side while keeping the circle stationary, all the radial lines would not tally, their lengths would differ.

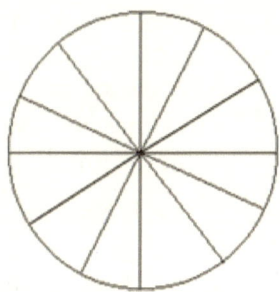 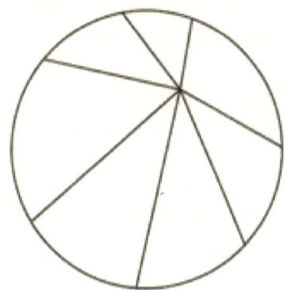

In the same way, when we operate from the center of our being, all our decisions prove to be right. Everything tallies in our life. The center here implies abiding in the experience of the Self, our true nature. Then we live life being the Source. However, if we shift our point of reference to a false identity other than the Self, nothing will tally in our life.

When we live life assuming that we are the body, we are divided into the various roles played by the body. We get so involved in playing these roles of being a daughter, a mother, a sister, a sister-in-law, a brother, a father, a son, a friend, a doctor, a lawyer, an actor, and so on that, we are unable to return to our true nature.

In a circus, you may have seen an actor wearing the costume of a lion, pretending to be a fake lion. The lion roars and shows his claws at the audience. The audience is entertained, but the person hiding behind the lion costume does not forget his true identity for a moment. He may walk, roar, and behave like a lion, but internally he knows who he really is. In the same way, no matter what role we perform, we should have a strong conviction about who we truly are. To develop this conviction, persistently question yourself, "Who am I?"

Let us understand this in detail. When you become angry, ask yourself, "Who is getting angry?" You will get the answer, "The mind is getting angry, then who am I?" This question will lead you to your true nature. When your face turns red in anger, your body temperature rises, it trembles, your nostrils flare; ask yourself,

"With whom is all this happening?" The answer will arise, "This is happening with my body-mind. I am different from it."

When you feel sad, question yourself, "Who is feeling sad?" You'll get the answer, "The mind is feeling sad." Ask yourself, "Then who am I?" You will feel a sense of detachment from the mind.

Suppose you are sitting on the shore of a pond. Your reflection is visible in the water. If someone says, "Look, your reflection is trembling," then what will you say? You will say, "Let the reflection tremble. I am not trembling." With the same clarity, you should be able to say, "The mind is feeling sad, not me. I am separate from the mind."

Your true Self can never be sad. Can you say that there is dry water in a glass? No, the glass can either have water or be dry. There is no such thing as dry water. In the same way, your true nature is happiness. How can it be sad? It is just not possible! How can light be darkness? Darkness is experienced in the absence of light. Darkness cannot exist in the presence of light.

When you say, "I am happy," you assume yourself to be the mind. But when you say, "I am happiness," then whom do you consider as 'I'? Close your eyes and reflect on this for a minute. When you say, "I am happiness," all the false masks you wear fall off; all the labels you have affixed on yourself collapse. You attain a state that is free of all labels. It is your true nature, beingness, the experience of Self. Just think, how often do you say this? Surely not often, because to be able to say this, you must dwell in that experience.

The experience of the Self is unbroken happiness without a cause. Love, peace, joy, enthusiasm, and liveliness are its qualities. Therefore, when you abide in the experience of the Self, you are endowed with all these qualities automatically. **A person may need reasons to be happy, but happiness is complete in itself without any cause.**

When you ask, "Who am I?" who is asking that? Is the body asking, or the mind or the intellect? None of them! The one asking this question is the answer to it. Only that which is alive can ask this question. The one who is asking this, you are that.

## "Who am I" - The great mantra

The question "Who am I" works like a great mantra. Use it every day to constantly remind yourself of your true nature. Make it a habit for yourself. Before playing any role, like a brother, sister, mother, father, teacher, or doctor, ask yourself, "Who was I so far, and who am I now?" Whenever you feel any sorrow or distress, ask yourself, "Who was I a short while ago, and who am I now?" Keep asking this question to yourself repeatedly throughout the day and keep remembering your true nature.

By force of habit, you may act from the assumption of being the body, but like a sword drawn from its sheath, use the great question, "Who am I?" to repeatedly cut through the assumption of the false 'I' and dwell in the experience of the Self.

You may have heard the story of the demon Bhasmasura. He performed arduous penance to please Lord Shiva and asked for a boon, "Whosoever's head I place my hand on should be reduced to ashes." Lord Shiva immediately granted him this boon. Now he decided to test this boon on none other than Lord Shiva! He ran after Lord Shiva to place his hand on his head. Lord Shiva had to flee, and Lord Vishnu had to incarnate as Mohini to save Lord Shiva. Enchanted by the beauty of Mohini, Bhasmasura started dancing with her, mimicking her every dance step. Then Mohini deftly placed her hand on her own head. Imitating her, Bhasmasura also placed his hand on his head, and sure enough, he was reduced to ashes.

Mohini's dance symbolizes Self-inquiry. You place your hand on the false 'I'. The demon of the "false I" dies in this inquiry. The way Bhasmasura became the cause of his own death by putting his hand on his head, Self-inquiry uses the mind to fell the mind itself, and the true Self, which was always present, is revealed.

## 10

## The Self's Mirror – The Body-Mind Mechanism

*You have to grow from the inside out.*
*None can teach you; none can make you spiritual.*
*There is no other teacher but your own soul.*

~ Swami Vivekananda

There is a unique village surrounded by a circular wall. The outer surface of this wall is made of mirrors. While going around the border of the village, one can see one's reflection in the mirrored wall. But the catch is that there are random holes in this mirrored wall.

Imagine you're walking towards this village. You want to see yourself in the mirrored wall. But as you go closer to the mirror surface, you notice the holes made in the mirror. Curious about what lies inside, you peep through the holes. Now instead of seeing yourself in the mirrored wall, you start watching the village scenes inside through the holes.

You see some people lying down, some sitting, some working. Among them, you also spot your duplicate – someone who perfectly resembles you. Now, you ignore everyone else and begin to focus on your duplicate. Like a detective, you spend all your time knowing everything about him – where he goes, what he does, who scolds him, what upsets him, when he gets angry, etc. After a while, you're so engrossed in pursuing the happenings of your duplicate that you forget that you are standing outside the village! You also forget who you are as you begin to believe that you are this duplicate. Everything that happens to the duplicate affects you as if it's happening to you.

Let us understand the deeper nuances of this analogy. Your duplicate in this analogy is your body-mind mechanism; it is the mirror. The holes in the mirrors are your senses, such as eyes, ears, nose, tongue, and skin. You are the Self beyond the body-mind. The whole and sole purpose of associating with your body-mind is to experience yourself by using your body-mind as a mirror. But as you get associated with your body-mind, you become so distracted by what you perceive through the senses that you forget to experience yourself. You get entangled in the colorful world attached to your eyes, ears, and nose. The three-dimensional world associated with your body and senses seems real to you. You get so mesmerized by this world that you begin to believe that you are this body-mind.

Blood flows in your entire body, but do you feel wet within? No. If you are the body, you should feel the wetness of blood. Do you feel the stickiness of blood and flesh? No! You experience yourself as being dry because even though the body is yours, you are not the body. However, as you get identified with the body, you feel whatever is happening with the body-mind is happening with you.

Why are we unable to have the purest experience of our true Self? Let us understand this. When you thread flowers with a needle, a third thing, a garland, is formed. Similarly, when the Self gets associated with the body-mind, a third thing—the contrast mind—appears due to their confluence. The contrast mind is that facet of the mind that compares, judges, and labels everything. It divides everything into good-bad, more-less, superior-inferior, etc. The false notion that appears due to the union of the Self with the body-mind forms a separate individual, the ego, which then functions as the contrast mind.

The contrast mind bewilders the Self and does not allow It to experience Itself. Thus, the glue of the contrast mind keeps the Self stuck to the mirror of the body-mind. Gaining an understanding of the Self and repeated self-inquiry of "Who am I?" act like a thinner for the Self to distance Itself from the mirror and experience Itself. It is only then that the purpose of the human body-mind is fulfilled.

When you sleep at night, you lose the sense of the body. It is as if the body does not exist at that time. You have no account of that time. You don't even know what happens to your body while you are in a deep sleep. However, when you wake up in the morning, you regain the sense of the body and assume yourself to be the body. Having lived with the body-mind for so many years, the belief "I am this body" is firmly established in your mind. Therefore, the moment you wake up from sleep, the experience of the body begins, and so do thoughts. What a tendency this is! How can this be broken?

Let us understand this with an analogy. In the stream of life, you are journeying by boat. The boat is your body-mind, and you are the boatman, the Self. In the presence of the Self, the body-mind comes alive, moving through the stream of life. You can have both the experiences – the experience of the Self and that of the body-mind. However, the contrast mind does not let it happen. For this to happen, it is necessary to surrender the separate individual that is formed. The individual does not really exist, but it appears to be present. When it becomes quiet, you can experience both the experiences—of the Self and the body-mind—very clearly.

Let us practice a meditation to understand how the sense of body and the sense of beingness (the experience of the Self) are simultaneously going on and how to identify and distinguish them. Read the following instructions before you practice the meditation.

**Two-Experiences Meditation**

1. Be seated in a meditative posture and close your eyes. Keep your body straight but relaxed.
2. Slowly, start breathing in a rhythm and experience the stillness within.
3. Now, experience the sense of your body as well as the sense of your being.
4. First, sense the body. Pay attention to all parts of the body. Notice which part of your body feels sore or tight.
5. If you feel pain or discomfort in any part of the body, experience that sensation.
6. Notice how the atmosphere affects your skin. Experience the warmth or cold feeling on the skin.
7. Whatever sensations you feel on the body—pain, discomfort, or sweat; experience them with this understanding that these are on the body, not on me.
8. Now focus on your thoughts. What kind of thoughts are running in your mind now? Are they happy, sad, or neutral? Whatever they are, just observe them.
9. Now experience your feelings. Do you feel peaceful within or anxious and restless?
10. Ask yourself, "Am I this pain and discomfort?" You will get the answer, "No, this is happening to my body." Then ask, "Am I these thoughts or feelings?" The answer will arise, "No, these are part of the instrument that I am using as a mirror to experience my presence."
11. The body-mind is journeying through time and space. Both the experiences are happening concurrently, but they are different. The first experience is that of your beingness, your living presence, and the second is that of your body-mind mechanism. Realize this difference.

12. Right now, you are experiencing the sense of being alive. The body-mind is also making its existence felt at the same time.

13. Both the experiences are happening at the same time. But the association with the body-mind has been there since a very long time. Hence the experience of the body-mind is felt first.

14. As you continue to shift towards the experience of the Self, you begin to develop conviction that you can dwell in the experience of the Self even while experiencing the body-mind.

15. If you lose awareness during meditation, question yourself again, "How many experiences am I having now? Who am I between the experience of the body and that of my being alive?" Let me dwell in that which I really am.

Open your eyes slowly. Try to dwell in this experience even after getting up from meditation. Abide in the experience as much as you can.

Let us understand some profound aspects. Initially, the seeker feels that the experience of the Self is possible only when the sense of the body vanishes, when the thoughtless state arises. But gradually, one realizes that the experience persists even if these things remain. If you realize the experience of the Self, you will not have any objection to the experience of the body-mind. You may say, "A while ago, I was able to experience the body and mind, but not now." Both the states are the same for you. A while ago, there were thoughts, but not now. If you are able to experience the Self, then the desire to omit the experience of the body or thoughts will end. You will not find any difference between the thoughtless state or the thought-filled state. In reality, who you truly are is indifferent of these states; your nature remains untouched.

The same thing applies in the case of emotions as well. You may feel, "If my body-mind is angry, then how can I experience the Self?" Let us understand it this way. If you are standing in front of a mirror and the mirror becomes hot, then will you experience discomfort? No! You will say, "So what if the mirror has become hot!? I am still able to see myself in it." Similarly, regardless of whether the body-mind is sick, healthy, angry, or at peace, it can still become instrumental for you to realize your living presence – the Self. With the consistent practice of meditation, as you become increasingly familiar with the experience of the Self, you will find it easier to understand and abide in it.

# 11

# The Face of Enlightenment – Behind the Seven Masks

*With realization of one's own potential and
self-confidence in one's ability,
one can build a better world.*

~ The Dalai Lama

As we have seen in the previous chapter, a separate individual comes into being when the Self gets associated with the body-mind. This separate personality keeps the Self identified and attached to the body-mind. The Self cannot experience itself through the body-mind until this attachment breaks. This separate personality wears various masks to maintain its existence. How can this attachment break and the Self experience itself? Let us understand this through an analogy.

Troubled by many problems in his life, a person left home and set out for the forest. He lost his way as he was roaming around. While trying to find his way back, he stumbled upon a unique tree. Rays of light were emanating from the tree. He felt drawn by an invisible thread as he went closer to the tree. As he caught the tree trunk in an embrace, he burst into tears. He then felt light and relieved, as if all his sorrows had dissolved; all the negativity in his mind had evaporated.

He was overjoyed. As he wondered about this miracle, he heard a voice coming from the tree. "Now that you're relieved of your sorrow, you can return home." The person replied, "How can I go back? I have lost my way. Even if I find my way back, what's in store for me at home? Everyone is so negative there. There are so many troubles and unsolved issues. I won't be able to live there." The tree assured him, "Do not fear. I am the tree of masks. I am giving you seven masks. Wear them when you deal with people. All your problems related to your relations will end." The tree continued, "But remember to return these masks to me next year." The tree then told him the way back home. Glad about this proposition, the person happily returned home.

The masks were transparent, and one could see through them. The person used all seven masks. While dealing with people, he would choose the mask depending on the context. He would wear the first mask while dealing with a single person. He would wear the second mask while dealing with a group of people. He would use the third mask when he met a stranger. He would wear the fourth mask when he would meet an acquaintance. When he would meet a true friend or a close relative, he would wear the fifth mask. He would use the sixth mask while meeting an adversary or rival. When he was alone by himself, he would wear the seventh mask. He would take off all the masks while going to sleep at night.

Thus, he started spending his life in a relaxed manner. He became an expert at switching the masks. He could easily get all his work done. He achieved success and started living much happier than before. In this manner, one year passed by very fast. He forgot that he had to return the masks to the tree.

With the passage of time, he started falling sick frequently. He sought various therapies but was not getting cured. Finally, he heard about a doctor and visited him. The doctor checked his pulse and advised him, "Your pulse is very strange. If you can trust me, your remedy is with a Tree of Masks in the forest. You should go and embrace this Tree of Masks and eat its leaves. Though it is rare to find this tree, if you wish to get healthy, you will need to do this."

The mention of the Tree of Masks astonished this man. At once, he remembered the tree that had healed all his troubles more than a year ago. He felt as if the tree was speaking to him through this doctor. He immediately traveled to the forest, held the tree trunk in a tight embrace, and asked for its forgiveness. "I did not return the masks on time as promised. Please forgive me." He continued, "Due to these seven masks, I have achieved a lot of success in life, started living happily. But I wish to learn how I can live after returning these seven masks, how will all my work get accomplished."

The tree said, "You just need to surrender your eighth mask, and everything will fall into place." The person was surprised, "The eighth mask?! Where did this eighth mask come from?" The tree said, "The eighth mask is the one upon which you have been wearing these seven masks. In deep sleep, you remove the eighth mask as well. But while dreaming, you wear it again." The person was bewildered upon hearing this new thing. He asked, "How will I get to know about this eighth mask?" The tree replied, "By practicing meditation. When you will witness all your masks and reflect over them in meditation, the eighth mask will automatically begin to fall off."

Let us understand the deeper meaning of this story. Whether we know it or not, we wear many mental masks while leading life in the world, dealing with people. We do not realize that the manner we speak and behave changes depending on whom we are dealing with. Our life is fragmented amidst these multitude of masks. By getting habituated to shuffling these masks, we have distanced ourselves from our true face—the face of the Self.

Contemplate: What mask do you wear in front of your boss? The mask of politeness. What mask do you wear in front of your subordinates? The mask of authority. What mask do you wear in front of your friends and acquaintances and with strangers? You treat those with whom you have a deep relationship with love. On seeing your adversary or rival, the masks of pride and hatred come to the fore.

Some people carry around more than seven masks! They feel the need to wear other masks on top of the eighth mask. Therefore, it is essential to surrender this eighth mask – the mask of ego. The eighth mask is your identification with your body, mind, and personality. You have mistaken it to be 'I.' The real face of the Self is mask-less, faceless, and formless.

Taking the story further, when the person sat under the tree in meditation, as the day dawned, he realized the futility of it all. He clearly saw how and where his seven masks were being used, how he was benefitting from them, what benefits he was attached to and couldn't do without, what the eighth mask was, and what state he would attain after removing it.

Seeing the futility of it all is the moment of eureka when we realize that we are wearing some mask or the other for more than sixteen hours a day. Even while dreaming, we put on the eighth mask to dream. After all, the one who watches the dream is your personality. Therefore, even then, at least one mask remains.

So, whenever you feel worried, ask yourself, "What mask am I wearing right now?" Remind yourself of the face of the Self. Throughout the day, ask yourself from time to time, "Which mask have I put on my face right now? What intoxication am I under?" You will come to know that some mask or the other is always put on. Once you realize this, you will be able to take it off easily. You will then feel the joy of being in the face of the Self. Bear in mind that this is not something to be experienced once, but rather you should live in this face, in this conviction of who you truly are.

Many questions arise in the seeker's mind when he lives a faceless life. For example, "If I live in the face of the Self without wearing any mask, will people accept me? How can I be successful in this world? How will I deal with people? How will I engage in third-person conversation? How will time be spent without a mask? Will I be able to enjoy life?" and so on.

The missing link here is that all these questions arise from the eighth mask! The mask itself raises doubts about liberation from the masks! At such time, understand that you don't need to solve or answer these questions but rather dissolve them! When you realize that all these thoughts arise from the mask, and not from who-you-truly-are, all these doubts and questions will dissolve at once!

You need to act without forgetting your true face. If you forget your true face—the face of the Self—and spend this lifetime without remembering it, then you have paid a very heavy price—a price that cannot be valued in terms of money. One who can truly assess the diamond can alone determine its value. He will say, "Do not lose this diamond. Human life is precious. Don't put it at stake. Realize the face of the Self and learn to lead life by dwelling in it. Sit with yourself and contemplate the obstacles you face. Decide to lead a faceless life."

Those who are incompetent wear more masks. As one becomes more competent, the number of masks reduces automatically. Here, incompetency implies the tendency of identifying with thoughts and emotions that are asssumed as 'I'. Now, these thoughts and emotions become one's master and drive one's life.

Let's assume your neighbor bought a new car. Externally, you wear a mask of congratulating him. However, you feel incomplete and jealous of him that you lose your sleep. This is incompetence. If you are clear about "Who am I?" you will be self-reliant and won't need to wear such masks. How can this competence be developed? It will develop with true knowledge. It will free you, give you courage, and make you brave at heart.

Consider for a while; if you are wearing the face of the Self, how would it be? It will certainly be free of fear, greed, jealousy, anger, and ignorance.

You need to be one in a million, not the millionth one. The millionth one is the one who follows the herd and gets deceived by the mask. The one in a million is he who dares to choose his own path and operates without a mask. This is the state of Enlightenment.

# PART 3

# ENLIGHTENMENT – TRUE FREEDOM

We are unable to experience true freedom as we remain stuck in bondage. Due to the attractions of the illusory world, tendencies, countless layers that shroud our true nature, various defilements, wrong assumptions and beliefs, and incessant desires, we are lost to the state of Enlightenment that was naturally available to us in our infancy.

This part unravels the path to true freedom. In this part, we will understand the causes of bondage and the secret of the real and fake ego. We will discuss the hindrances that aggravate bondage and the ways of freeing ourselves. We will discover the secret of realizing the bliss of true freedom.

# 12

# Understanding the Ego

*Ego is the primal sin;
greed, anger, and desire its shadows.*

~ Sri Ramana Maharshi

There is a very subtle veil between individual existence and the state of Enlightenment. It is the ego. The permanent dissolution of the ego is Enlightenment. Hence, understanding the ego is an essential step in progressing towards Enlightenment. Many accomplished seekers do not understand the play of their ego due to which their lives do not flow freely.

Life is like a flowing stream. The beauty of a stream is in its flow. Despite numerous obstacles, it finds its way through them and flows ceaselessly. It is only because of this free flow that its beauty prevails. The ego is an obstacle that can diminish the beauty and rhythm of life. Hence, we should understand exactly what the ego is and how it manifests in everyday life.

**Real and fake ego**

To understand the subtlety of the ego, it can be differentiated into two parts.

1. **The real ego** - When one identifies oneself with one's body, mind, and intellect, naturally, one assumes oneself as an independent entity. One regards oneself as separate from others as well as nature. This is the real ego or the root ego. It is the subtle feeling that "I am separate from the rest of the creation; I am separate from all other beings." Separateness is at the core of the real ego. This is not easily discernible. It is the root cause of the illusion.

2. **The fake ego** - The fake ego is an offspring of the real ego; it stems from the root ego. When one considers oneself a separate individual, one considers oneself special and superior to others. This is the fake ego. Obviously, the fake ego is bound to follow in the footsteps of the real ego.

The real ego begins to form in a child after the age of about two-and-half to three years. A feeling of "I am separate" begins to arise within him. All the members of the family tend to him and pamper him. They bring him new clothes, sweets, and toys. As a result, he starts considering himself as an important entity. He does not understand that he is still small and physically delicate, so everyone pays extra attention to him.

As he grows, along with the real ego, his fake ego also gets boosted and also feels hurt on trivial incidents. Perhaps he went to someone's house and wasn't offered a chair to sit. Someone made a belittling face and walked away. The teacher ignored him in the class. A friend neglected him. He did not perform well in a competition. He was overtaken by someone while driving. Not one, but there are a multitude of reasons due to which the fake ego can feel hurt from morning till night.

The fake ego can be easily recognized as it manifests itself as anger, boredom, confusion, depression, fear, greed, hatred, ill-will, jealousy, and lust. These vices are expressions of the fake ego. However, the real ego, being very subtle, is not easily grasped. It is hidden and not obvious.

The biggest missing link is that most people assume their fake ego to be the real ego. As a result, the real ego goes unnoticed. People work hard to get rid of their fake ego but never succeed. Even if they are able to subdue the fake ego for some time, it rises again, because the real ego is hideously still alive.

Consider a tree that has a big trunk and some branches. The ego is the trunk. Anger, hatred, or greed are the branches of the tree. Most spiritual practices attempt to work on the individual branches; tackle them individually. The drawback with this approach is that when one branch is severed, the other branch shows up. When we try to control a particular vice, say anger, another vice overpowers us. This is like a snake with multiple heads. When one head is severed, it raises another ugly head.

In the Indian epic, the Ramayana, Lord Rama tried to kill the demon king, Ravana, by shooting arrows at the ten heads. But every time a head was severed, a new head would replace it. However, when Lord Rama shot the arrow at his navel (the root), the demon-king met his end.

This story is symbolic. The ten heads represent the ten vices. Shooting at the navel implies uprooting the entire tree, instead of trying to cut down individual branches. We need to tackle the root of the tree – the real ego. When the real ego comes to an end, all the vices automatically dissolve. They cannot exist without the root ego.

When we consider ourselves separate from others, we get attached to the body-mind. We consider ourselves superior to others and expect attention and respect. Once we understand this, we work in the right direction. Only when we fire the arrow at the right spot will the Ravana within us die.

## Service of the ego

The fake ego makes people constantly strive to prove themselves better than others. In this struggle, their minds are often overwhelmed with doubt, anxiety, and restlessness. To unwind their minds, some people resort to alcohol, some gamble, some watch television, while some others instigate fights between others for no reason. Thus, they keep gratifying the incessant demands of their minds. This has been called the service of the ego.

Suppose someone is abused by their neighbor. Their mind immediately provokes them to retaliate. Their mind becomes quiet only when they have given back to the neighbor in the same coin. This is nothing but slavery of the ego.

Somebody has guests visiting their house, and their child is creating a lot of noise, "I want this; I want that." He puts his hand in the cookie jar; he pulls out a bottle of juice. His parents think, "The child is being stubborn. Let us give him what he wants for the time being. We will lovingly make him understand and get rid of stubbornness later after the guest leaves." But that "later" never comes. Over time, the stubborn child grows, and so does his stubbornness. Then his parents say, "We have given up on him. He just doesn't listen."

So it is with the ego. The ego arises every now and then right from when we wake up in the morning till we sleep at night. It provokes, annoys, and torments. No one likes such a disturbance and restlessness. They think, "Let us do something for the time being to pacify the mind for now. We will figure out a permanent solution later." But that "later" never comes. This amounts to serving the ego. It is time to seek a permanent solution to be free from the ego.

**Action Plan**

1. **Make the right choices**

    Often, we come across such situations in life where we have to choose between two options. They could be major or minor decisions in life. For example, you plan to go on vacation and have to choose from two options - Kashmir or Goa. So, you extend two fingers towards your friend and ask him to pick one finger. In your mind, you have already decided that the shorter finger is for Goa and the longer one is for Kashmir. When your friend picks the shorter finger, you accept that and say, "Alright! I will go to Goa." You have to adopt precisely the same approach in every incident. Ask yourself, "Whom do I favor? (a) The ego, or (b) Love, joy, and peace (facets of the Self)?"

    If someone scolds you, the ego will retort, "You should scold him too." But now you will pause and ask yourself, "What holds priority in my life? (a) The ego, or (b) Love, joy, and peace?"

Whenever the ego raises its head, your alignment with the Self is disturbed. You get overwhelmed with anger, humiliation, and sorrow. At such times, ask yourself, "In whose favor do I choose to work? (a) The ego, or (b) Alignment with the Self?" If you are a true seeker, you will choose option (b). In this way, keep asking this question in all incidents from morning till night, and you will spend your entire day in awareness. This exercise will safeguard you from the service of your ego. You will work in favor of the Self.

2. **Know the real Self**

    Keep asking yourself, "Who am I?" after short periods. This will raise your level of awareness. As you become aware of who you truly are, the fake ego will not be able to throw tantrums and create turmoil.

    The real ego is that facet of one's consciousness from where all vices arise. False personality, countless desires, stray thoughts, baseless assumptions, wrong beliefs, misunderstandings, sensory temptations, tendencies, and detrimental habits arise from the real ego. The real ego is the root of all of this. When the real ego is tackled, all of this fall apart. When we witness our true nature in meditation, we start watching our thoughts and emotions from a distance. This loosens the grip of the real ego.

    In this section, we will work on becoming free from the tendencies, beliefs, desires, and misunderstandings that stem from the fake ego. We will understand our true nature and the false personality, how we can free ourselves from the double personality and stabilize in our true nature so that we can experience the joy of total freedom.

    When practiced, the techniques given in the following chapters will ease your path to Enlightenment.

# 13

# The Trick To Avoid Getting Tricked by the Senses

*One may conquer a thousand men in a thousand battles.*
*But he who conquers just one person is the greatest conqueror.*
*He who is self-restrained has tamed his self;*
*nobody can turn such a victory into defeat.*

~ The Buddha

Human beings are bestowed with the gift of five senses – eyesight, hearing, smell, taste, and the sensation of touch. We can make these senses instrumental for attaining Enlightenment. We perceive the world through the medium of these senses. The senses play an important role in keeping the body and mind healthy.

If any of them do not function properly, we find it difficult to go through our daily chores. For example, if our tongue does not function properly, we will not know the taste of the food we eat. The same is the case with our other senses. If our ears, eyes, nose, or skin don't function properly, we will be deprived of those sensory experiences and pleasures. Therefore, we should put this blessing of the senses to good use.

The problem arises when we become attached to the content of the senses. For example, the purpose of the tongue is to identify the taste of the food and perceive whether it is sweet, bitter, spicy, or salty. And the purpose of food is to keep the body healthy. But how many people bear this in mind when they consume food? Not many! Most people eat food to gratify their craving for taste. They give more importance to taste than to nutrition. When the food is delicious, they consume it in excess, more than the body needs.

Thus, keeping aside the actual purpose of the senses, they get lured by the temptations of the senses. They crave to see enchanting sights through their eyes, hear melodious music through their ears, enjoy tasty food through their tongue, pleasant fragrances through their nose, and experience soft touch through their skin. Gradually, they get so used to sensory pleasures that they rebel when they are deprived of them. They become restless and commit wrongdoings. Ideally, they should put their senses to proper use and make them instrumental for Enlightenment.

Losing ourselves in sensory pleasures is like eating chocolate without removing the wrapper. When one eats chocolate with its wrapper, one does not enjoy its real taste. The experience is subdued. The joy derived from sensory pleasures is similar. It may seem pleasant, but the truth is something else.

Why do we seek sensory pleasure in the first place? It is because we seek happiness in the wrong place. We fail to recognize that the happiness we experience in sensory pleasures is already present within us. We wrongly connect the happiness that is experienced with the objects of sensory pleasure. The more we experience such misplaced momentary happiness, the more convinced we are that we can obtain happiness from worldly pleasures. This leads to the formation of a tendency to chase after sensory objects.

If one savors two sweets today, the mind craves to have the same taste tomorrow. If one relishes the fragrance of a flower today, the mind demands to have it tomorrow as well in greater measure. It will also imagine, "I wish I experience the fragrance of many other varieties of flowers too!"

Thus, the desire to satiate the senses is dangerous as it later forms a tendency. If one is praised, one feels momentary happiness but aspires for more praise. If one is thirsty, one feels his thirst can be quenched after drinking some juice, but it is not so. Thus, people increase their dose of sensory pleasures and in turn get entrapped in the deception of sensory enjoyment. They get stuck in deriving happiness using the wrapper of sensory delights. They fail to do away with this wrapper and cannot make the senses instrumental for enjoying the causeless bliss that lies behind it. As a result, they feel discontented.

Whatever happiness they receive is wrapped in the layers of sensory pleasures. Now, these layers need to be removed with the help of wisdom. Once the layers are removed, you will say, "So much happiness was always already present within me, but I was not aware of it. Being alive, the sense of beingness, is a reward in itself. It is a cause for happiness. Then why should I seek any other reward!?" There is potential for such a great transformation!

You may have heard the story of Mother Ahilya in the Indian epic Ramayana. Sage Gautama cursed her that she would turn into stone. When Lord Rama's feet touched the stone, she came back to life. This story holds a deep meaning. Contemplate whether any such curse is at work in your life as well, like that of Ahilya. A life can be considered cursed if it is trapped in inertia, if the mind and intellect have become rigid. In such a state, one keeps getting more ensnared in the deception of the senses. Even if a tiny stone in the form of the slightest inertia develops within us, we should still be wary. This one stone can retard the flow of life into a stone-like existence, even if everything else is fluid. Only Lord Rama, in the form of higher awareness can pull us out of this inertia.

The senses deceive us due to the hidden desires within us. Also, we fall prey to temptations and become restless when we do not get to enjoy them. Sensory attractions can be very deceptive. The Indian epic Mahabharata depicts this through the character of Yudhishtira. Despite being wise and virtuous, he had such a weakness for playing dice that he staked his kingdom, wealth, and even his valorous brothers while playing dice with Duryodhana. Despite everyone's advice, he finally staked his wife, Draupadi. This is the extreme height of inertia, where he became so oblivious that he paid no heed to his conscience and the advice of his dear ones.

There were no mobile phones in those times, and the technology was also not that advanced, so the opportunities of getting entangled were also lesser. Still, the senses could deceive them. Today, there are innumerable avenues that are available at our fingertips that can entice our senses. Therefore, we need to be extremely alert.

We cannot stop the world from inventing such gadgets or services that make the internet accessible to children at their fingertips at a tender age. Instead of blaming these merchants of sensory attractions, we should rather invest our time in making ourselves vigilant by asking, "How am I living from morning till night? Are my senses leading me towards inertia?"

The earlier a seeker on the path to Enlightenment realizes that "Only clean water quenches thirst, not any carbonated beverage," the better. Once we realize that the contentment derived from sensory pleasures is false, we will not want to live this lie. Then transformation can happen.

**Action plan to safeguard yourself from the deceit of the senses**

On the one hand, we need to progress by using the medium of the senses, while on the other hand, we need to become aware of our weaknesses. We can progress towards Enlightenment by making good use of the senses and avoiding their misuse.

1. **Use the senses as a medium**

    Those who aspire for Enlightenment need to be aware of their weak areas through which temptations can infiltrate and get ingrained in the mind. Our senses are dual in nature – they can serve us in our journey to Enlightenment, and they can also enslave us.

    You need to experiment and find out which of your senses are most receptive. For example, if your sense of hearing is predominant and you like music, you should deliberately listen to such divine music that helps you abide in your heart. This way, you can use your senses as a medium. On the other hand, if you listen to fast-paced ear-splitting music for superficial entertainment, that would be the misuse of senses, as it will excite and entangle you.

We need to bring such awareness in all aspects of life – our livelihood, skills, expression, body, health, relationships, service, and surroundings, so that our senses do not become a curse for us.

2. **Increase real happiness**

Belittling others to feel superior, mocking someone, laughing at others' problems, etc. are examples of false happiness. When we indulge in these cheap ways of deriving second-hand happiness, we misuse the senses. To safeguard ourselves, we should boost the real happiness in our life. This will loosen the grip of senses on us.

For example, if you are going to attend a family function, resolve to see only virtues in the people you meet; openly appreciate their virtues; stay away from criticism and backbiting. When you reach the venue, leave aside your old habit, and behave as you have decided. The happiness you will experience will be pure and real. It will be far superior to what you would experience by indulging in gossip and criticism. This is an example of putting your senses to good use.

Initially, one experiences pleasure in receiving, but slowly one realizes that the joy of giving is much greater. Seeing the twinkle of happiness in others' eyes expands real happiness. This is a different state in which one is no longer eating the chocolate along with the wrapper. One is able to see one's past foolishness clearly. With this, the topics of the senses begin to lose their grip on us. The mind begins to turn inward and dwell in the essence of devotion. One starts deriving happiness from meditation, listening to the Truth, contemplation, singing devotional songs, and divine veneration. Having learned superior methods of being happy, one would no longer wish to pursue inferior pleasures.

# 14

# Being Neutral to the Stress of the Senses

*Liberation is in your hands as soon as ignorance ends.*

~ Anonymous

In the previous chapter, we learned about the web of sensory pleasures. We will now discuss the stress that comes from sensory indulgence. If we don't work on the cravings and aversions of the senses, we find ourselves overpowered by stress due to the senses. Cravings and aversions do not let the senses be at peace. Hence, we are always stressed about doing something or the other all the time.

When the senses run amok and cause the stress of indulging in sensory content all the time, how can we remain in the present? We are always preoccupied with thoughts like: "What has happened to my friend's result? I should quickly call him and find out. What is the breaking news today? When will I read the newspaper? What will be the outcome of my interview? What gifts will the guests bring?" and so on.

The drama of the senses continues even when we meditate. We become preoccupied with thoughts like: "When will this meditation get over? When will the bell ring? When will I reach home? I have to complete these activities upon reaching home," and so on. Our senses race ahead to the future.

Due to this tendency of racing, our mind is always pulled by the senses. Consider someone turns on a vacuum cleaner close to our eyes. It is as if the hose of the vacuum cleaner is sucking us. Something similar happens to us. We get pulled automatically to wherever our senses drag us. This is craving. And we also try to escape certain other things that our senses avoid. These are aversions. We are pushed away from some things while being pulled towards some other things. We are sucked from someplace and blown towards someplace, leading to stress.

Imagine, if a single desire is like a vacuum cleaner, then considering our innumerable desires, how many vacuum cleaners can push and pull us in different directions? How tense will the mind be in such a state?

Once this tendency of racing after sensory objects is formed, we do not realize that we are in a tensed state. It becomes a new normal for us. Thus, we get used to a tensed state of mind. This is nothing but hell. If one is staying in hell, but is used to it, there cannot be a worse hell than this, because one never gets the thought of coming out of this hell!

As the human mind gets bored with the status quo, the senses always seek something new to eat, see, and listen. The anticipation of joy in watching a new movie or wearing a new costume causes excitement. These days, when people get fed up with the same house, neighbors, people, and things around them, they seek novelty in the world of social media. They await new posts, new videos, and status updates of their contacts. The demand to conform with digital social groups pressurizes one so much that sometimes the stress manifests in the form of physical ailments in their body. They get afflicted with diseases.

In such a state, it is essential to forcefully tell the senses, "You are not going to do anything now. For some time, there's neither the need to know something new, nor ask for something new, nor become impatient for something."

In the stories of Krishna Leela, Lord Krishna is shown sitting in absolute peace on the banks of the Yamuna river playing his flute. Here, Lord Krishna symbolizes pure consciousness. The tune that plays from this state of equipoise fills both living beings and non-living objects with love and calm. The senses no longer wander without direction. They are in a state of perfect rest. In other words, they obey the command of Krishna consciousness as opposed to doing whatever they please. The more the senses become introverted, the more they align to the divine will.

To attain Enlightenment, the seeker's senses should be like that of Krishna, where there is no attempt to know something, nor is there a search for something new. In that state, the flute is not played to escape boredom, but it's played from the state of rest itself. When Meera dances in the temple or on the streets, while remembering Krishna, she is not doing so out of boredom. Her dancing is not the result of her slavery to her senses but rather an expression of her liberation! She dances in divine ecstasy.

However, if anyone without such a disposition is asked to sit in a neutral state for a while, the mind will question, "What will I gain by sitting this way?" If he is told that he will become enlightened, he will be stressed and start worrying, "When will I get enlightened? It has not happened yet. Will it ever happen?" In short, the stress caused by the senses prevents one from dwelling in the state of perfect rest and expressing oneself naturally. God expresses only through those bodies that are empty like a flute. If one is afflicted by tension and worry, how can one decode God's guidance!? Only a relaxed, peaceful, balanced, and neutral body can attain the purpose of life on Earth and attain Enlightenment.

Those who have Enlightenment as their goal need to practice being detached and stress-free. The neutral state is an internal state of indifference to the push and pull of the senses. It is a disposition where the chaos of the senses ceases, and so does the tension that arises from it. There is no interference from the senses to whatever nature presents in the now.

**Action plan to be in a neutral state**

1. Take advantage of opportunities to get a short break from work or your daily chores. For example, if you are waiting for someone's call and you have nothing else to do, you can practice a neutral state with awareness during such time.

2. When you are home and not working on something important, close your eyes halfway. This position of the eyes will help you remain detached.

3. When you are idle, pay attention to the attempts being made by the senses to get something—to see something, feel something, hear something, change something, or taste something. Mere observation without judgment will help you be in a neutral state of indifference.

4. Remember the tortoise as the symbol of the neutral state. When a tortoise is at rest, it tucks in its head and all its limbs within its shell. When seen from above, it is difficult to tell that there is an animal there; it becomes so still. Imagine this picture of the tortoise to tuck in your senses in this manner.

## 15

# Overcoming the Delusion of Two Paths

*The difficult problems in life always start off being simple. Great affairs always start off being small.*

~ Lao Tzu

Indraneel visited his friend Amar for a dinner party. There were two types of dishes being offered—one for those who were fasting and the other for the remaining people. As Indraneel was not on a fast, he relished the non-fasters' delicacies. Amar assumed that Indraneel was fasting and insisted that he partake of the fasters' diet. But instead of clarifying that he was not fasting, Indraneel enjoyed the best of both the types of dishes.

Just like Indraneel, if a seeker of Truth also enjoys being stuck between heaven and hell, then he is indeed in a dangerous state. It will lead him astray from the journey to Enlightenment.

Some people dwell in hell, which is a good state. Some others dwell in heaven, which is an even better state. But there are people who dwell in a third state between heaven and hell. This is the dangerous state of delusion.

One might ask, "I can understand that being in heaven is a better state; but how can being in hell be a good state?" When we are stuck in our habits, tendencies, and preconceived notions, and if we are aware that we are stuck, then we are in hell. We would even want to get out of this hellish state but perhaps find it difficult right now. In short, we have clarity about our present state.

Similarly, when we have already worked within ourselves and attained a state of equanimity and virtuousness, we are in heaven. We realize that we are in a much better state, but we wish to progress even further to the transcendental state beyond heaven and hell.

Both these categories of people – those who dwell in heaven and those who dwell in hell – are aware of their internal state. One wishes to come out of hell, while the other wishes to progress further beyond heaven. However, one who is stuck between heaven and hell, dwells in delusion and leads an oblivious life. In this delusion, they want to take advantage of both heaven and hell, without realizing that they first need to get rid of this delusion, choose one side and progress towards the transcendental state.

The transcendental state is the experience of the Self – the essence of our beingness. It transcends all dualities and attributes. In this state, we become free from both heaven and hell and dwell in the state of Enlightenment.

**Understanding the delusion**

It is essential to first understand the delusion to get rid of it. Quite often, one wants the best of both worlds. For example, one may feel good by engaging in gossip and cheap humor. At the same time, they also like to listen to discourses on the Truth. This means they want something from hell as well as from heaven.

While leading a worldly life, one comes across many alluring temptations. He feels good indulging in them. For example, he keeps hearing that life is worthwhile only if he becomes famous, arranges for his child's higher education in an esteemed university abroad, attains a high designation, or leads a luxurious life. He gets overpowered by these ideas on the one hand, while on the other hand, he strengthens the will to attain Enlightenment after attending spiritual discourses.

The illusory Maya keeps convincing him, "There is great fun in taking credit for every successful task you accomplish. What difference does it make if you take a little bit of credit!" Then someone praises him, "Wow! How do you manage to accomplish so many things so efficiently?" Even though he knows very well that everything is happening by divine grace, he is unable to let go of the joy that comes with taking credit for whatever happens.

Similarly, in the journey to Enlightenment, a seeker knows that it is important to put the knowledge of wise words into practice instead of merely acquiring and flaunting it. And yet, he is unable to give up the joy of posing as an erudite scholar and impressing others with his bookish knowledge.

For a seeker whose objective is to attain Enlightenment while his body is alive, it is useless to vacillate between Maya and Enlightenment in such a state of delusion.

If someone is suffering in hell, he automatically starts praying for liberation. But the thought of liberation doesn't arise in one who is stuck between heaven and hell. He enjoys the benefits of both. Sometimes he considers himself the physical body, while sometimes, he considers himself the Self. When he relishes delicious food, he considers himself the body; otherwise, he won't be able to enjoy it. So, he wants to remain in this confused state so that he can enjoy his favorite food. He thinks, "I'll dwell in the Self when I experience some physical discomfort. Let me enjoy this now." In this way, on the one hand, he uses his body to experience his sense of beingness, while on the other hand, he becomes the body to indulge in sensory pleasure.

He does not understand that sensory pleasure shrouds true happiness in such a way that everything becomes clouded. Therefore, it is important to understand this delusion.

If you feel an itch somewhere, scratching makes you feel good, but it only worsens the itching sensation. As soon as you understand this, you won't scratch it even if it feels good but would rather treat the itching sensation or bear with it for a while so that it subsides on its own. Similarly, when one is deluded and unaware of it, one indulges in the trap of sensory pleasures.

When one is able to clearly appreciate the true happiness, he can experience on being free from this delusion, he will then progress to transcend it and dwell in the essence of the Self. It is only because one has not fully experienced the happiness of being free from delusion that he wishes to remain in the false joy of delusion. He fears that he will be deprived of worldly pleasures if he were to be freed from his delusion. He is afraid of how he can survive without praise, credit, and the pleasures of the senses.

It is important to realize our delusion to go beyond it. We need to contemplate the matters in which we are a victim of delusion. Do we enjoy being in the state of ignorance and misconceptions? Or do we feel miserable being in such a state? If it pains us to lead a life of ignorant bliss, that is good news.

There is a phrase known as "pig's contentment" that means the blind pleasure that pigs experience while rolling in sludge. Similarly, do we experience pig's contentment by indulging in sensory pleasures? If it feels enjoyable to indulge, we should contemplate whether it is true happiness. Where will it lead us?

A salesman used to walk from door to door in housing colonies to sell his goods. He was tired and thirsty, but nobody offered him water for drinking. Suddenly a woman came out of a house and invited him.

Earlier, the woman's husband had called her from his workplace to inform that one of his friends would be visiting. The woman who had never met this friend, mistook the salesman to be her husband's friend and welcomed him. She greeted him warmly, offered him a glass of juice to drink and snacks to eat.

The salesman had his doubts, "Perhaps this woman is mistaking me for someone else." But he didn't bother to clarify because his logical mind reasoned, "Let her dwell in this misunderstanding. My fatigue and hunger are being taken care of. What else do I need? If I tell her the truth, she'll kick me out. If she finds out later, I can always tell her that it wasn't my fault that she mistook me for someone else."

Thus, in the guise of an excuse that seemed logically right, the salesman enjoyed the hospitality that was not due to him. He was encouraged by the possibility that no one would ever find out. It is good that Saint Meera did not entertain such thoughts.

Saint Meera's husband, Rana Bhojraj, who was the chieftain of the kingdom of Mewar, warned her, "If you don't stop attending spiritual discourses, meeting saints, or worshipping Krishna, I will banish you from the royal palace." Saint Meera remained steadfast with the Truth despite these warnings. She could have lied to him, "Fine, I will no longer worship Lord Krishna," and continued to enjoy the luxuries of the palace.

She could have continued silently worshipping Lord Krishna in her heart without outwardly expressing any form of worship. By doing this, she could have enjoyed the comforts, the grandeur, the fine silks, jewelry, delicious food, and adornments of the royal palace, and her worship of her beloved Lord Krishna would also have continued. But Saint Meera chose the Truth. She became doubtlessly ready to willingly abandon all the royal comforts and pleasures for the sake of the Truth.

When Sudama, the bosom friend of Lord Krishna, was suffering in abject poverty, he and his family had to often go without food. Yet, Sudama stayed firm with the Truth. One of his friends had advised him, "You sing so beautifully in veneration of Lord Krishna. If you were to sing in praise of our king, he will surely reward you with enough wealth to end your poverty." But Sudama refused to let his tongue sing praises of anyone other than Lord Krishna. Infuriated by this, the king admonished and penalized Sudama harshly, but Sudama did not give in. He refused to stray from the Truth.

Saints like Meera and Sudama remained firm and resolute with the guidance they received from their Self. They never compromised on their conscience. They were never in the state of delusion—oscillating between heaven and hell—but always remained established in the divine essence of pure beingness.

One who is liberated from delusion leads a life of integrity. His feelings, thoughts, speech, writing, and actions are always aligned to the Truth. In other words, his outward conduct perfectly reflects his internal state. There is no deceit or dubiousness. He doesn't intend to take undue advantage of other's innocence or ignorance. He is the same within and outwardly.

The state of pure beingness transcends both "inside" and "outside", both "inward" and "outward". This transcendental dimension of Oneness encompasses all other dimensions. In other words, it is the root or source of everything. By abiding in this root state of the Self, one can clearly witness the play in all dimensions and hence, consistently make the perfect choice in every situation.

Outwardly, the actions of these exalted souls could defy practical reasoning. People wonder, "What did Jesus gain by giving up himself to crucifixion? What did Saint Meera gain by relinquishing the royal palace? What did Saint Dnyaneshwar gain when Saint Nivruttinath instructed him to write the Dnyaneshwari? He had to write such a large volume! Was this suffering or enjoyment?"

**The joy experienced in fulfilling God's will is boundless and beyond logic. These souls were experiencing such divine bliss in being instruments for the divine will that for them everything else paled in comparison.**

The logical mind cannot reason this. It believes in having the cake and eating it too! In its state of delusion, it tries to take advantage of both Maya as well as the Truth. So as an earnest seeker on the journey to Enlightenment, we need to be determined to get rid of this escapist approach of treading on two boats at the same time.

### The hurdle of the logical mind

While living in delusion, one trusts one's logical mind. He considers the logical arguments of the mind as the gospel truth. He does not doubt their validity even a bit. From the absolute standpoint of the Self, these arguments are baseless. To understand this, one should be detached from his body and mind and realize the sense of pure beingness beyond both. When he perceives from that absolute viewpoint, he will see the flaw in the mind's logic. He will realize, "What I believed to be happiness is not really so."

Consider that you decided to attend a spiritual retreat on a particular day, and you receive a phone call from your friend on the same morning. He insists you to attend his birthday party. Now your logical mind reasons, "I should accept my friend's invitation. I can always attend this retreat next time as I cannot displease my friend." Such a choice is made because you consider yourself as your body-mind. However, if you perceive from your beingness without attachment to your worldly roles, you will then make a different choice altogether. You will choose to safeguard yourself from the influence of Maya and fulfill the divine will. You will realize the futility of the mind's logic.

You cannot attain Enlightenment by choosing the best of both worlds. Hence, you need to become one-sided. For that, work upon the following action plan.

### Action plan for freedom from delusion

1. **Prioritize your goal**

   First, write down the goal of attaining Enlightenment while the body is alive in your diary and always remember it. Set highest priority to it. **Firmly decide that everything else will be secondary to achieving this goal.** Come out of the illusion that mere superficial effort can help you attain Enlightenment.

   Read inspiring biographies. **Swami Vivekananda's objective was so powerful that it became the driving force of his life** and resulted in his magnanimous expression. First, you need to empower this goal; then, the goal empowers you. Then no obstacle can impede you. A powerful goal is complete in itself. It gathers energy from all unproductive channels and focuses you to remain steadfast on the goal.

2. **Honestly, give yourself the proof of contemplation**

   If the state of confusion between heaven and hell is being misused as an excuse for enjoyment, make a list of all the things you enjoy today. Then contemplate whether it is real joy or an illusion of joy? Investigate each item one by one. Give yourself the testimony of your contemplation, "Whatever I regard as happiness today, how is it misguiding and impeding me from attaining true happiness? Staying in delusion gives me temporary pleasure, but should I continue on this path, or should I choose the path to Enlightenment?"

# 16

# Liberation From Multi-layered Existence

*Those who searched by diving into deep waters found the treasure.
I foolishly feared drowning and kept searching on the shore.*

~ Saint Kabir

The journey from a multi-layered existence to becoming free of all layers is a key aspect in attaining Enlightenment. If we can comprehend this through direct experience, then Enlightenment is just around the corner!

This chapter throws light on the multi-layered existence of human life and the path to freedom from layers so that you can get rid of the layers that have gathered over your existence one by one. Indeed, you deserve to be congratulated for having reached this far!

When we fold a big sheet of paper in half, a layer gets created. As we keep folding, more layers get added, and the sheet shrinks in size. Imagine a sheet of paper as large as the earth. How many layers will be formed if we keep folding it!? Human existence is also like such a multi-folded sheet of paper. There are innumerable layers of mental conditioning created on the sheet of awareness within human being that are invisible. Imagine human being is like a compact disc. If the sheet of awareness were unfolded, all the layers would dissolve, and one just cannot imagine how vast the fully unfolded sheet can be!

Due to ignorance and lack of awareness, we keep creating new folds in our life, thus forming layers upon layers, one over the other, with every incident we encounter. If someone speaks to us loudly, we get angry with him. If someone ignores us, we draw conclusions about why he would have done that. Every time an incident occurs, we form opinions about it and judge it as good or bad.

Can you imagine how many layers you have stacked within!? As we keep consciously unfolding and removing these layers one by one in a deliberate manner, we move towards being established in pure awareness – the state of Self-realization, free from all conditioning. This state is already always present but has remained obscured due to the accumulation of so many layers on top of it. It is like the peels of an onion. If you remove the peels of an onion one by one, the "nothing" that remains at the end is the layer-free state.

**The creation of layers**

A newborn child does not have any layers. He is the purest expression of the Self. But as he grows up, he gets conditioned through upbringing. He gets trained on adding layers by his parents, siblings, teachers, neighborhood, and the social media. The very first layer is that of the separate individual 'I' that gets formed over the pristine nature of the Self. With this layer, a separate individual entity appears. When the child is about two and a half to three years old, he begins to identify himself with the body-mind by holding onto the body-mind's name, gender, community, nationality, religion, physical features, etc. This is how the first layer of the personalized 'I' gets formed and builds further. Later, many layers get added one by one over this first layer.

Let us understand this with the help of an example. Our true nature is like a ball, and the first layer of the individual 'I' is like a double-sided sticky tape fully covering our true nature on all sides. The inner sticky side of the double-sided tape is stuck to our true nature of pure awareness. The outer sticky side of this tape is open, upon which other layers like "mine," "your," "their" get stuck. In this way, our true nature gets covered by numerous layers of labels, beliefs, and notions. In the end, this cascade of accumulating layers takes on such a gigantic proportion that we are lost to our true nature completely.

Let us see how the game of layers could possibly begin. On the child's first birthday, the family gifts him a beautiful dress. However, he is least interested in wearing new clothes. But as he grows older, he cries if he does not get new clothes on his birthday. What brings about this change? Layers of conditioning. Gradually, he develops the habit of adding new layers with every incident.

Parents, relatives, teachers, neighbors, and others keep adding to the layers in the lives of children by continuously feeding them with limiting beliefs. These beliefs could be, "Life is difficult," "People can betray you," "It is not so easy to make money," "If you laugh too much, you will have to cry too," and so on. On hearing this repeatedly, the child develops fear, starts deceiving others, and gets engrossed in the habit of creating layers. This thick shroud of layers pulls him away from his pure essence. As a result, he digresses from the state of Enlightenment.

In school, children write with chalk on a writing slate. When one child sees something nicely written on the other's slate, he purposely erases it by wiping it with his hand. The other child gets angry and gets even with him by erasing what's written on the first child's slate. He says, "You erased my writing. Now I have also erased yours." Thus, they form yet another layer on top of their true nature. And the series of such incidents goes on. Their pure nature gets contaminated with folds when they engage in comparison, deceit, and jealousy.

As the child grows up, more and more layers get formed within him by the bitter-sweet experiences that he goes through, the influence of the ideologies of the people around him, observing what others do, and his own commentary during incidents in his life. The commentary could be, "Good that this happened," or "What happened was very bad; it shouldn't have happened," or "Someone should avenge what happened," and so on. There is so much that is buried within a person – past burdens, fixations, programmed reactions, wishful thinking, suppressed negative emotions, injured memories. There is so much baggage! All these together form a thick shroud of layers around one's true nature.

The state of pure awareness that was present in the child at birth is shrouded by the constant formation of layers. The layer-free state of supreme bliss is indeed gifted to all of us at birth, but we are lost to it as layers get formed within the body-mind around our pure presence.

In the material world, scientists are striving hard to explore space travel, uncover the hidden secrets of galaxies and oceans. No matter how many of these external secrets are unraveled, these achievements cannot help one un-fold the layers within and become truly happy. One can derive true happiness only when one is able to reveal the mysteries within oneself. Those who journey inward can open the folds within.

## The layer-free state of pure awareness

For those who aim for Enlightenment, un-folding the layers within and attaining the layer-free state of pure awareness is the key aspect in the journey. Hence, it is important to understand the game of layers in depth.

Consider the state of one who is filled with innumerable layers, whose inner voice has been suppressed, who has drifted away from his true nature, and who keeps burning in the fire of hatred, resentment, jealousy, and spite.

It is not that happiness can be experienced only after all the layers are removed. As each layer un-folds, we can experience a faint sense of the joy of freedom. We begin to increasingly experience happiness. We will be pleasantly surprised, "Earlier I used to be troubled in this situation, but nowadays I am able to effortlessly accept it and be at peace." With the un-folding of each layer, resistance dissolves and acceptance rises, due to which the quantum of happiness increases. It is unimaginable how blissful we can feel on opening up fully and removing all the folds that caused these layers.

When the fundamental layer of the false 'I' is un-folded through the process of intense sadhana, we reach the Buddha state. When the Buddha un-folded the fundamental layer of the false 'I,' he attained the state beyond the mind. In other words, he transcended the conditioning of the body-mind and was established in pure awareness, which always existed. In this experience of the Self, pure awareness is experienced not just within and outside the body-mind, but beyond it. This is the undivided state of Oneness beyond all forms of duality.

**Action Plan**

1. **Attaining the layer-free state by practicing forgiveness**

   After reading about layers, given that there are far too many layers within, one might perhaps lose hope that un-folding all of them seems almost impossible. But there is no need to fear. It is possible to un-fold them all. The easiest way to be free of layers is the practice of seeking forgiveness for liberation—*Mokshama*. Yes, you can attain liberation by practicing forgiveness!

   Seeking forgiveness does not mean that you are blameworthy. It only means that you are taking responsibility for inner cleansing and paving the way to Enlightenment. This is a powerful technique to get un-folded. For this, you need to seek forgiveness from God and pray for inner cleansing.

   Seek forgiveness from the bottom of your heart. The more heartfelt the plea for forgiveness, the greater the possibility of un-folding the layers and flattening the folds of mental conditioning.

   The water of forgiveness acts as a thinner to loosen the bond of glue of the first layer of the individual 'I'. As a result, the thick shroud of layers formed over it begins to crumble and fall off. For this, we can offer the following prayer as a practice of Mokshama -

   1. "O God, please forgive me. Please cleanse me from within. I forgive everyone. May everyone forgive me."

2. "I have unknowingly harbored wrong beliefs, created many layers, continued to remain constricted, and shrouded the immaculate state that you had bestowed upon me in my childhood. Please forgive me for this."
3. "The sheet of awareness is being cleansed. It is becoming pure. The magic of forgiveness is working. I ask for forgiveness from the bottom of my heart. Forgive... forgive... forgive..."
4. "Every breath, every plea for forgiveness is un-folding me. I am opening up. I am blossoming like a flower. I am becoming more and more relaxed."
5. "O God, Thank You for opening me up. Gratitude for all your mercy. Thank You for your divine grace."

In this way, you can erase each layer by seeking forgiveness for it and letting go of it. The regular practice of forgiveness will speed up the un-folding process, and soon you will begin to experience the layer-free state.

## 2. Letting go of the layers with breathing meditation

Meditation on the breath is also an easy way to let go of layers. Breathing is ongoing all the time. It is always available to us. Therefore, we can take its benefit to attain a layer-free state any time.

1. Close your eyes and be seated in your chosen meditative posture. Take a deep breath and exhale slowly.
2. Sense that the incoming and outgoing breath is helping you to un-fold. Focus on your breath with the feeling that "I am opening up with every breath."
3. Every breath is an unspoken mantra. Lord Buddha started his journey to attain the layer-free state by meditating on the breath.
4. Observe the breath coming in and going out. With every incoming breath, visualize that the layers are getting removed one after the other. With the outgoing breath,

visualize that the folds or creases formed due to these layers are getting erased.

5. Keep un-folding at your own pace. You are neither in a hurry nor are you feeling lazy. Neither are you lethargic, nor are you hyperactive. You are merely attending to your breath, which is un-folding you.

6. Your breath is always with you. Open yourself with the breath whenever you feel constricted by thoughts of fear, limiting thoughts, future predictions, or difficulties.

Open your eyes slowly. We will understand more about layers in the next chapter. With every chapter, you are being given various techniques. Identify the one technique that works best for you and practice it. This practice will help remove what's unnecessary and reveal your true nature.

# 17

# Getting Rid of Wrong Beliefs

*To attain Enlightenment, you have to be simple,
you cannot make it by being complicated.
One must remove all the knots and become innocent.*

~ Anonymous

In the last chapter, we learned how one gets entangled in the process of adding layers. The false and limiting beliefs hidden in the subconscious mind make these layers even deeper, and the deeper these layers are, the greater the suffering. Thus, a vicious cycle of beliefs, layers, and sorrow keeps self-perpetuating.

A seeker of Enlightenment must break this vicious cycle. Let us understand this cycle in more detail in this chapter so that we can work to become free of the layers with the right understanding.

## Wrong Beliefs

Only two things can happen in human life—one is the reality, and the other is belief. **Whatever is actually happening in life is reality, and whatever the mind feels should not be happening is belief.**

Since childhood, we have been conditioned by numerous beliefs that constitute our present mindset. Though this conditioning is far from the Truth, it is deeply ingrained in our subconscious mind. Due to these wrong beliefs, we get stuck in the extremes of happiness and sorrow and keep adding layers upon layers over our true essence. Whatever is happening is the reality, but the mind can hold the belief that it should not happen. By resisting whatever is happening, we experience sorrow. Howsoever much we try to change the world around us; it is these beliefs within us that cause sorrow.

We tend to focus more on "what should not happen" instead of "what is really happening". We think, "I shouldn't lose my job," but we do. "We shouldn't fall ill," but we do. If we honestly contemplate, we will see that we experience unhappiness due to the notion "I shouldn't have lost my job" than actually losing the job. If one is suffering from knee pain, more than the pain, he feels hurt due to the notion, "This is so painful. It shouldn't be there." If his neighbor throws trash in front of his house, he is more upset due to the notion, "He shouldn't have done this." **More than any incident, it is the belief that there should be no sorrow, that actually causes sorrow.**

Man does not suffer single sorrow, but double sorrow! When an undesirable incident occurs, he suffers sorrow by resisting it. Additionally, he also suffers double sorrow by brooding over the first sorrow, "Why am I suffering? Why am I unhappy? Until when will this go on?" This habit of suffering double sorrow has developed within us due to deeply ingrained limiting beliefs. Due to this habit, the layers do not just get added, but get multiplied.

For example, if one experiences physical discomfort for some reason, he keeps thinking, "I hope this isn't a heart attack. I am still too young for this. This isn't time for me to say goodbye to the world. I hope I don't die soon." As such thoughts gain momentum, it deepens his suffering and adds more layers within him. People inadvertently cultivate many such sorrows.

Imagine what will happen if you get rid of all layers? While you may experience pain in the body, you will see that there is no sorrow due to the pain. In other words, you accept the pain as it is. Pain is the body's feedback. If you use your body for a long time, your body is bound to give feedback. If there are changes in the diet or weather, your body will signal it through sensations. For example, if you work longer for a day, the body will tell you, "I'm exhausted today. It's paining me." So, you will seek medical advice and tend to the body, but without brooding or adding any layers.

You may perhaps have seen little children who get badly injured. They are unable to lift their leg due to the injury, but they keep laughing about it. They find it funny that they are unable to move their leg because they clearly understand that they are not the leg. This scene becomes quite funny.

Why can the child laugh at the injury? Because until then, there's no layer created in the child's mind that says, "Pain is bad, it shouldn't happen. If this pain aggravates, anything can happen. I will not be able to walk. I will not be able to run. I will not be able to earn a living. I will not find the right partner. I will be handicapped. People will look at me with pity." As the child does not harbor any such beliefs, he is able to laugh while he is in pain.

Some beliefs are deeply ingrained within people. For example – "If you haven't achieved this milestone in life, how can you sit still? You haven't built a mansion yet. Your daughter is yet to be married. Your son still hasn't found a good job. You haven't gone on a world tour yet. Then how can you be happy?" When people meet, they discuss such topics. Listening to them, one could lose heart and start believing that life is worthless without such achievements. He may perhaps vent out his frustration on his family, thus creating layers of conditioning.

In this way, people keep creating layers in the name of honor, respect, religion, caste, and creed. These deep-rooted beliefs trouble them so much that they are prepared to kill and die for these beliefs.

Contemplate – From morning till night how many situations make you unhappy. Your unhappiness, in itself, implies that you are trapped by beliefs. If these situations repeatedly happen in your life and you suffer sorrow, it means there are layers within you.

Understand this. As one keeps adding layers, sorrow is created. That there should be no sorrow is also a belief. If sorrow is helping you identify the beliefs within you, how can sorrow be bad? It is bringing your beliefs to light and helping you progress towards liberation. Therefore, it is an important milestone for the seeker to be free of the dangerous belief of lamenting over sorrow.

As a child, you had no wrong beliefs. You were living a simple, natural, and intuitive life, like a blank sheet of paper. But the experiences you had in the world have created beliefs within you. Let us understand how beliefs enter our lives.

## The basis of beliefs

### 1. The experiences in life

The experiences in our life form the basis for our joy and sorrow. Repeated experiences create a substratum for joy and sorrow. Without this substratum of past experiences, joy and sorrow cannot stand by themselves!

A bowl is filled with water and a piece of paper is placed on the water surface. The paper is so thin that it will be submerged if something is placed on it. Slowly, the plain piece of paper starts gathering experiences. With every experience, a fold is created in the paper. Now, as the paper has many folds, if something is placed on it, it can firmly support it. It is the same piece of paper as before, but where did this firmness and strength come from? It came from the folds, from the beliefs that got ingrained through the experiences gathered.

Let us understand with one more example how experiences turn into beliefs.

A cute child is walking along the road. People start teasing the child in jest. Somebody pulls his cap off while someone else snatches his bag. The poor child starts crying in fear. Even though these people return his cap or bag after teasing him for a while, the child's experience makes him believe that anyone can harass him while he walks on the road. He also forms a mental image that those people are bad. One of them had curly hair and big eyes. Now, whenever he encounters someone with curly hair or big eyes, based on his prior experience, his mind unconsciously concludes that this person is bad.

## 2. Self-reporting or interpretation

Whenever an incident occurs, we try to interpret it, form an opinion about it, affix a label on it, whether it is good or bad, and fixate a reason why it is so. For every incident, we inadvertently do such reporting in our mind, without knowing what it will create in our life. We get entrapped in our own words and labels by reporting this way. It creates a belief or strengthens existing beliefs within us. While forming opinions, we do not realize how firmly they will get ingrained as beliefs within us.

Every day we keep reporting to ourselves within, "This always happens with me," or "These people will never improve, no matter how many times I explain to them," or "I can never perform this particular task," or "It is difficult to change one's nature," or "No need to attend spiritual discourses; just fulfil your duty to family and society," or "It is not so easy to attain Enlightenment," and so on. In this way, self-reporting done without consciously thinking or understanding reinforces the folds and strengthens the layers within us.

If one's friend remarks, "This sportsman is useless to the team," he immediately agrees. But do they reflect on it before passing such comments or agreeing? Just because he didn't perform well in one match, has he become useless? One should give careful thought before speaking. But when one has already said it, he sticks to it. He tries to prove it right and keep his belief intact.

Therefore, we should pause for a while before speaking and investigate, "Is this really the truth? Or am I misinterpreting it?" If we are honest with ourselves, we can save ourselves from creating further layers. Otherwise, we deceive ourselves through wrong self-reporting, and the layers within us become deeper. This is like a spider that secretes a web out of its mouth and then gets trapped in its own web!

## 3. Popular opinion

We tend to borrow the opinions of people around us. When this happens repeatedly, people's opinions become our beliefs and determine our joys and sorrows. For example, if the family feels, "Until one attains a certain higher designation in the organization, one cannot earn respect," we firmly believe this, thus creating a layer within us that craves respect through promotion. The power of beliefs goes to such an extent that it not only makes us unhappy during this lifetime but also makes others unhappy. In the normal course, it never occurs to us that all these beliefs are unnecessary. We spend life suffering such sorrows that we never really deserved.

Today, social media is playing a significant role in influencing popular opinion. With increasingly more screen-time, the younger generation is vulnerable to being influenced by the social media, given that it is easily accessible and extremely potent in creating deep impressions in their mindset. Seekers who wish to journey to Enlightenment need to be vigilant not to let social media influence them. If one continues to indiscriminately indulge in social media, one can get all the more entangled in the quagmire of beliefs and form more complex layers within them instead of moving towards freedom from all of this.

## 4. Reference point

Our life is governed by a reference point. All our thoughts, opinions, and perspectives are based on this reference point. Imagine what can happen if this reference point, in itself, is wrong? All our thinking, rationale will come to a naught. All our assumptions and judgments about people, situations, incidents, and life at large will prove to be wrong. Unfortunately, this is the underlying cause of all the sadness, conflict, struggle, and disharmony in our lives. We live our life based on a skewed point of reference.

When we start totaling a series of amounts – say for reconciling accounts – if the first amount is incorrect, then we is bound to get the total wrong, regardless of how accurately we perform the addition. Our calculations will never reconcile. Similarly, if our reference point in life is skewed, then every decision and judgment in our life are bound to go wrong. Things will never add up in life, and we will never be able to reconcile with life's situations.

Let us take an example. Rational thinking tells us that most people around us are unhappy for some reason or the other. We cannot find a single person who is completely and unconditionally happy and fulfilled, no matter what. We see people making compromises in their lives – be it their career, marriage, or giving the best to themselves.

For example, people tend to be dissatisfied with their marriages to varying degrees. Seeing all this, one anticipates a similar fate for oneself too. This is a wrong belief that gets harbored owing to a faulty reference point. There is no chance of altering this deeply set belief unless we find the right reference point.

When the world learned about the Buddha's teaching that there exists a state that is free of sorrow, they found a new reference point. Without the right reference point, how can they develop faith in the experience of the Self? Therefore, seek the right reference point. Seekers of Enlightenment should search for an advanced seeker or a true Guru who can help redefine their reference point, so that they can develop faith that Enlightenment is possible in this very lifetime.

**Action Plan**

**1. Improve the original script**

While treading the path to Enlightenment, it is important to first correct your original script. Otherwise, one keeps making corrections in the copies of the script. Never make this blunder.

The simple meaning of correcting the original script implies taking responsibility for everything that is happening in your life. Most people tend to blame what seems to be going wrong on others, or situations, or their fate. However, the original script of your life is present within you in the form of your beliefs and inclinations. When we change the original script within us, we begin to experience the reflection of these changes in our external world.

Without this understanding, one leads life with confused thinking and attempts to manipulate external situations and people hoping that things will turn for the better. This is like trying to make corrections in the copies of the script.

Working on your original script implies understanding and getting rid of wrong beliefs and assumptions within you, that have shaped your experience of life today. Reflect on every situation and look out for underlying beliefs and patterns within your mindset that could possibly be causing these situations to manifest in your life.

For example, a seeker firmly believes that "Whatever I say is right." This belief works in all areas of his life—his office, family and friends, and other seekers. As a result, he gets involved in arguments and disputes everywhere. He experiences disharmony in his relationships. People do not cooperate with him. Complications and standoffs keep occurring in his life. His life is spent in causing a mess and then reconciling it. He had set off on the journey to Enlightenment but gets bogged down in his tracks due to this fundamental belief, "Whatever I say is right."

It is essential for him to correct the original script within himself. He needs to see how others can be right, and how he could possibly be wrong. Such introspection will help him shake and uproot this belief. Situations will automatically change for the better the moment he releases this belief.

## 2. Challenge your beliefs

Challenge all your beliefs that cause sorrow. When you challenge any belief, new possibilities come to light. For example, you are unable to find a job. You are unable to find the right life partner. Can getting the right job or finding the right partner be real reasons for happiness? Challenge these beliefs and see for yourself. Look at the lives of those who seem to have the "perfect" job or the "perfect" life partner. How long does such happiness last?

Once, a palmist studied the lines on a person's palm and said, "You will never get married." The person asked, "What makes you say so?!" The palmist smiled, "Because your lines show that you are only destined for happiness!"

Well, this was a joke. This certainly doesn't mean that people should not get married. It only means that we should not base our happiness on our notions of "that perfect partner." A youth once approached the Greek philosopher-seer Socrates and asked, "Should I get married? Please advise me." Socrates laughed, "Either way, you will be unhappy!"

Socrates meant that we invite unhappiness by holding onto our beliefs about what can make us happy. You need to challenge your beliefs. "Can this really give me lasting happiness—a job, a person, an incident?" In this way, you will need to challenge your beliefs and give yourself evidences of their fallacy.

Britney Gallivan from California challenged that a sheet of paper can be folded more than seven times. Those were times when it was assumed that a paper cannot be folded more than seven or eight times. She challenged this belief and proved that a piece of paper can be folded twelve times. Similarly, Galileo challenged the popular belief that the moon has blemishes. He said that the moon does not have blemishes but has mountains and craters.

These were examples of assumptions about the external world that were challenged. However, many Self-realized souls have challenged such beliefs that helped people get liberated from their sorrows. The Buddha's life is a message to the world that a sorrow-free state is indeed available in each one's life.

It is immaterial whether you get answers on challenging your beliefs. The important thing is to develop the habit of challenging your beliefs. Tell yourself, "Whatever I consider bad, could it possibly be good." You can surely give this challenging thought the benefit of doubt.

First, you need to be sure that you want to live peacefully with ease. If you are unsure about it, you will always find yourself entangled in beliefs. Therefore, be firm with yourself. Be committed to attaining Enlightenment in this life itself.

# 18

# The Garb of the Fake Personality

*Those who wish to sing always find a song.*
~ A Swedish proverb

Imagine you have a special dress which is your favorite. You were gifted this dress long ago, and you chose to wear it. When you wore this dress, you weren't fully aware of the consequences of wearing it. However, when you wore it and stepped out, some flies began to come close and stick to it. Some of them started stinging you, while some others started tickling you.

However, if you leave your house in your night-suit instead of this special dress, these flies don't stick to you even though they buzz around you.

What is so unique about the special dress that flies get attracted? Unknown to you, there is some sticky substance on the dress that attracts these flies.

Wearing this dress symbolizes donning a special personality that attracts these flies. You never knew that all this while, the culprit was your dress. When you wear the night-suit, you don't take on any personality. You remain as you really are. Hence, nothing is attracted towards you. You can happily take a stroll.

Given an option to choose today, would you like to wear such a dress? Obviously, you will say, "I won't wear such a dress that attracts such flies that keep stinging or tickling me!" You chose this dress long ago and had been wearing it out of habit. As a child, one may like some things, but he need not necessarily like the same things as an adult. He may not even need them later. Given this, how sensible is it to choose the same dress just out of habit?

## Who am I? Who is the personality?

Let us understand the deeper meaning of this analogy. What is the special dress? What are the flies? Why do they stick to the dress? The special dress is the fake personality, with which you have identified as 'I.' The Self—your pure and true nature—has draped this personality over itself. On wearing this dress, It forgets Itself and starts living as if It is this separate imagined personality, which does not really exist. The moment the unlimited Self becomes limited to this personality, the thought-flies begin to buzz around and stick around the notion of this personality.

Wearing the night-suit signifies being who you truly are. When you live by being who you truly are, the flies in the form of thoughts cannot trouble you or lead you astray. As the body is limited, a limited personality seems to exist, and as a result, various things are attracted towards it. There is a real 'I' and its reflection. The reflection does not really exist but seems to be there.

This illusory fake personality attracts things towards us. If we had not donned it, those things would not have been drawn towards us. And even if they did, they would not have stuck to us.

## As the personality, so are the flies

Whatever kind of dress you wear, that kind of flies are attracted towards you. Without realizing this, you believe, "This particular place has more flies. More flies appear when I am in the company of these people. Flies sting me more in these specific circumstances. Flies flock more during this period. If I can safeguard myself during that period, I can go through the rest of the day peacefully," and so on.

The truth is that flies in the form of thoughts don't get attracted towards us because of the outside environment but rather because of our dress. If we start living without this personality-dress, the thought-flies will disappear, or at the least, they won't stick to us. In other words, if we venture into the world as who-we-truly-are, nothing can draw us out of our blissful experience. We will wonder why aren't we suffering anymore!

## The role of attachment

In the analogy, there is a sticky substance on the special dress, due to which flies stick to it. This sticky substance represents attachment to the body. While living in the world, when we identify with the body, we fall victim to attachment due to which the body's desires are assumed as "my" desires.

Depending on the temperament of the body—lethargic, hyperactive, or equanimous—some thoughts occur in the body. The Self simply witnesses them. However, attachment to the body poses a hurdle in this witnessing due to which the thought-flies start sticking.

This stickiness is impossible when we lead a life of detachment from the body-mind. Wearing the night-suit symbolizes being detached from the fake personality. In the analogy, when we wear the night-suit, flies may buzz around but not stick to us. This means that when we are not attached to the body-mind, we can experience who-we-truly-are even in the presence of thoughts because thoughts won't stick to us.

## Who empowers this fake personality?

How is the fake personality? It feels good when it is appreciated. If someone criticizes it, it immediately tries to refute the criticism. It tries its best to defend and prove how it is right. In every incident, it says, "See, I told you this would happen. I knew it. Even though I have told them, people continue to do this. Then this is bound to happen," and so on.

By repeating this behavior day in and day out, one does not realize even once that, "I am empowering, pampering, and safeguarding a personality which is not who I am." To prove himself right and keep his personality intact, he even goes to the extent of hurting others. He feels pleased when he is able to prove that he, as the assumed personality, is right. When people acknowledge, approve, or appreciate him, his heart feels contented, so the game continues.

All these antics continue in the darkness of ignorance. Hence, he needs to understand that he shouldn't pamper and safeguard this personality that does not really exist but just appears to exist!

Thoughts are also part of this fake personality. When one feels disappointed or irritated, one starts blaming others. This is especially so if one is already disappointed or jealous of others for some other reason. One does not blame one's dear ones. This is all the drama of personality.

For example, if there is a bomb explosion somewhere, whether one becomes happy or sad depends on his attachment to that place. If the explosion happens in his native country, state, or town, he could have thoughts of concern. If it happens in a remote country, state, or town, his thoughts could be different. This difference in thinking is because of the fake personality. Depending on the place the personality has identified as "mine," he feels happy or sad about whatever happens there. He feels relatively indifferent to the places he does not identify with.

**Double personality**

In reality, we live with not just one but two personalities. It is like going about life wearing two dresses. The first personality is the limited personality that the Self has assumed Itself to be. It has assumed Itself to be the limited body, mind, and intellect. The second personality that derives from the first one is the worldly roles It plays due to which It assumes Itself to be these roles. First the body, and then on top of that, the various roles. In this way, the Self assumes a double personality.

For example, a woman thinks, "My son is not at par with other smart children. The world is not good. Anyone can outsmart him. How will he cope with competition?" She gets overwhelmed with sorrow and worry by immersing herself in these thoughts of a mother. Whatever role we play in the world, we become that. Indeed, this is the double dress.

## The stickiness of thoughts

By sticking to thoughts, man empowers them. Without this understanding, even a single thought can cause him to suffer for his entire life. Just imagine the risk of being in ignorance! A single thought has the power to shake him to his foundations. It could be any stray thought, such as, "Anything can happen in life. Death can come anytime. How will I survive when my parents depart? What will I do if I don't find a good job? How will I meet my expenses?" If such thoughts get stuck, it can trouble him for perhaps a day, or a week, a month, or sometimes even many years! Not just this, some thoughts can become the cause of sorrow for his entire life.

In ignorance, he continues to empower this personality. With every thought, something is being added to the personality. For example, if the thought of fear arises within him, a label gets stuck on the personality, "I'm a coward." Similarly, the thought of anger gives rise to an angry personality within him.

Setting aside this personality, if he remembers to ask himself, "Who am I?" and observes all his thoughts from that place, they won't be added to his personality. In this state, thoughts of fear will not create a coward. Thoughts of anger will not create an angry person. He will simply witness them, and the fake personality created due to thoughts will begin to dissolve.

## Leave the false personality

One cannot easily leave his false personality because he also gets tickled by wearing it. A little child may want someone to play with him and tickle him to have fun. But what if he continues to desire the same thing even after growing up? No, old toys drop off automatically when one gains understanding.

Today you are attracted towards liberation; you wish to live life peacefully. Therefore, clearly understand that unless the Self wears a personality and creates a fake 'I' (the ego), the flies of thoughts have no power. The mind should be convinced that it is safe to survive and thrive even without wearing a personality. The mind tends to be afraid, "How can I live without a personality? How is it possible? Nobody will listen to me then," and so on. Hence, you try to safeguard your personality at any cost. But if you wear the night-suit (living without the ego) even for a little while, the richness of that experience will inspire you to blissfully live without wearing the special dress of personality.

As you become aware of this mistake and work on it, you can easily distance yourself from your thoughts. Contemplate on how the personality gets created; what exactly do you take upon you that it comes into being? What knowledge do you need to stop this from happening? What witnessing and realization can help to make it happen? What are your weaknesses due to which you take on a separate personality without consciously being aware of it? Once you understand these subtler aspects, you will be determined to put an end to them.

**Action plan**

Let us understand how we can free ourselves from this fake personality.

**1. Strike at the root cause**

Those who aspire for Enlightenment need to work on the root cause. However hard they try to resolve their superficial issues; it does not yield the ultimate solution. They may stop thinking negatively and try their best to think positively. But as they suppress one negative thought, another one crops up. Thoughts may quieten for a while, but soon they rise again. People spend their entire life trying to get rid of negative thoughts but in vain. Hence, it is necessary to understand the root cause first and work on it. Considering oneself separate from others is the root disease that must be treated first. Thoughts arise due to the separate personality.

## 2. Act, but don't get entangled

Once you understand the game of the fake personality, you will play your role well while leading life in the world. After realizing your beingness, you just need to play out your role externally. It is just like a joker in the circus who knows his true nature and the purpose of his acting to entertain the audience.

Sometimes, you need to play a role in the world for which you may need to act for a long time or do so repeatedly. There is a possibility of entangling in the role at such times. Hence, awareness is very important. You should not forget, "I have taken on this personality to play a role for the benefit of others. My intent is very clear."

In this way, always keep yourself vigilant. This will keep you on the path to attain Enlightenment.

# 19

# The Aggregation of Impressions and Tendencies

*The secret of happiness is not found in seeking more, but in developing the capacity to enjoy less.*

~ Socrates

A clowder of cats was discussing who their leader should be. The bravest, most experienced, and wisest of them was chosen by consensus to be their queen. To honor her, she was crowned and seated on a throne with the offerings of fruits and flowers. The Ministers' court was held. Suddenly, a mouse scampered by the throne. And sure enough...

The Queen cat immediately jumped out of her throne and dashed after the mouse. While chasing the mouse, her crown fell off her head, but she was more intent on catching the mouse than safeguarding her crown. Despite receiving the highest honor, comforts, respect, and the royal throne, she could not hold herself back on seeing the mouse. What happened to her upon seeing the mouse that she forgot everything else? It was the powerful tendency within her to chase after mice and catch them. This tendency forced her to react despite her will.

Let us understand what tendencies are and how they function. When we keep doing the same thing repeatedly, we develop a tendency of doing it. After repeating it frequently or for a long period, the tendency takes the form of a deep impression. Thus, deep impressions are instinctive tendencies that largely govern our life. They guide and direct our life without our conscious control.

Those who have a cynical personality always harbor doubts about others. They see everyone with suspicion. Those who are daydreamers build castles in the sky. Rather than doing any constructive work, they keep swimming in the sea of their imagination. Yet others are very sensitive. They lament over minor happenings. In this way, everyone behaves according to their tendencies. Some lead their lives driven by ambition, fear, greed, anger, pity, vengeance, or a desire to gain spiritual merit. Their tendencies compel them to make such fixed choices.

**How do tendencies form?**

Let us understand how tendencies are formed. During summer, when the snow at the mountaintop melts and the water flows down for the first time, it carves a path for itself as it flows down. It strives hard to navigate through various obstacles in its path downhill. However, once the path is formed, the water easily flows through the same path for every subsequent snowmelt. Once the rainy season ends, the water beds dry up. But the next time the rain hits the mountains, the water flows down along the same channels. Similarly, one wants to do things in the same old way that one is used to. He takes the same path downhill every time, just like the melting snow.

In much the same way, once an action bears a successful fruit, it forms an impression and gets deeply engraved within us. For example, when we realize for the first time that we can quickly get our job done by scolding or shouting at our office staff, our mind fixes it as a formula for success. Then we start using this formula every day. Slowly, it becomes our second nature. In the process, the impression of shouting gets so deeply engraved that even if we don't want to shout, this tendency gets the better of us.

If these tendencies are not identified on time, they get so deeply ingrained within us that they can raise their heads as and when they get a chance even if we have this understanding. Hence, it is essential for seekers walking the path to Enlightenment to identify their impressions and tendencies and become vigilant. Understanding how these tendencies pose a hurdle in their path and how to get rid of them will help them attain the goal.

The story of Vishwamitra and Menaka is well known in Indian mythology. Sage Vishwamitra was absorbed in rigorous penance in an uninhabited forest. Indra, the King of the Gods, felt threatened by his penance and sent the celestial nymph Menaka to seduce him and disrupt his penance. Initially, Menaka could not influence him. But, after a while, Vishwamitra got distracted by Menaka. He broke out of his years-long penance and got drowned in her love. After that, he gave up on his quest for liberation. He got married to Menaka and started living a life of luxury.

How did such a great sage stray from his path? The reason is straightforward. Lust was dormant within him. Tendencies and impressions are such a raging fire that can reduce even rigorous practice to ashes. It is another matter that when Vishwamitra realized his mistake, he resumed his penance and attained Enlightenment. But he lost many years of his life due to a single tendency.

**Mental instincts**

If the repetition of habitual activities forms tendencies, even the thoughts we entertain repeatedly can give rise to mental instincts. If we constantly think ill of someone, it becomes a tendency. Often, one is unable to openly say or do anything in person to someone, but he harbors envy, hatred, and vengeful feelings for them. If this feeling intensifies, it becomes a significant obstacle on the path to Enlightenment.

Let us understand how tendencies shape one's life from the examples of Draupadi, a central character of the Indian epic Mahabharata, and Saint Meera, a devotee of Lord Krishna. Draupadi and Meera were both devotees of Lord Krishna. Both loved Lord Krishna unconditionally. However, Meera could attain Krishna consciousness through her love, but Draupadi couldn't. Draupadi even had the advantage of the direct company of Lord Krishna and his guidance in real life. Lord Krishna was her dear friend. On the other hand, Meera never met Lord Krishna in person, yet scaled the summit of supreme devotion.

What could be the reason? The reason was the instinct to seek revenge. Draupadi was born with the poison of vengeance. Besides, the fire raging within her to seek revenge against the Kauravas did not allow her to reach the summit of devotion to Lord Krishna. As she was not aware of this deep impression of vengeance within her, she did not take any steps to be free from it. This is the illusion created by tendencies and impressions.

Tendencies and impressions develop within us in two ways. One is by repeating the same tasks or thoughts, which we can be consciously aware of. The second way is through our DNA, from our ancestors, which we are unaware of. We naturally inherit the tendencies and impressions of our parents and grandparents. As in the example of Draupadi, she was the daughter of the king of Panchala, Drupad. King Drupad had procreated her through a fire sacrifice he had conducted with the sole intention of destroying the Kuru clan. In this way, the very purpose of Draupadi's birth was to seek revenge. She had naturally inherited this instinct from her father.

A seeker needs to identify both these kinds of tendencies consciously. When we progress on the path to Enlightenment, our trivial habits and tendencies get eliminated through listening to spiritual discourses and contemplation. But we need to identify and diligently work on the deeply ingrained impressions derived from old diehard habits and inherited from our ancestors. Our personality thrives on these habits and tendencies. Hence, it does not want to let go of them. So, they remain stuck to us like leeches. We learned from the cat's example that despite getting the royal throne, she left it behind to catch the mouse. Deep-rooted impressions and tendencies are like the mouse, making us give up our royal nature. They can drop us into the abyss of a lowered state of consciousness.

This is where sincerity, faith, and obedience to the Guru's instructions come to our help and can save us from these profoundly ingrained tendencies. With consistent efforts, prayer, meditation, and the practice of forgiveness, we can become free from them.

## Action plan

### 1. Be creative

A creative person never develops any tendencies because he chooses a different path every time. For example, a pickpocket stole a person's wallet that contained two thousand rupees. When the person realized that his wallet was stolen, he started clapping loudly. When he was asked why he was doing so, he answered, "I saved three thousand rupees today. I had five thousand rupees in my wallet. But before leaving home, I kept three thousand rupees in the cupboard." Rather than lamenting the loss of two thousand rupees, he looked at the situation creatively and saved himself from being sad. Moreover, he prevented developing a tendency that would have caused him sorrow. This is creative thinking. Besides this, we must become creative in our actions too. Sometimes by changing the order of activities, time, or technique, we can bring creativity to our work and prevent the formation of deep-rooted tendencies.

### 2. Recognizing the liberation zone

Let us understand in which stage of any incident liberation is present. Whenever an incident occurs, we respond to it. In between the happening of the incident and our response to it lies a small interval. It is called "the interval of freedom of choice." This interval, also called "Liberation zone," is so subtle that it is imperceptible.

We need to be sensitive to be able to recognize this subtle interval. The moment any incident happens, tendencies raise their heads and force us to react in the old ways. But before reacting, we need to become quickly aware to consciously choose the right response for the given situation.

You may ask, "How is it possible?" The liberation zone is short. You cannot even perceive it on the time scale you are used to. And yet, you must learn to catch this subtle moment. Practice being in the liberation zone before responding to any event. Ask yourself, "Can I respond differently despite my inherent tendencies and nature?" This question will inspire you to respond appropriately. Even a small conscious appropriate response is a big blow to your deeply ingrained tendencies. If you keep blowing them like this regularly, they are bound to break one day. Recognition of the liberation zone prepares you for attaining Enlightenment.

You need to shift your focus from the incident into the liberation zone. For that, practice raising your sensitivity and shifting your focus from the unfolding of the incident. If your focus is on the incident, your tendencies will manifest and start their antics. Your mind will remain entangled in complaining, increasing the chance of an inappropriate response. A liberated response backed with understanding will arise when you shift your focus away from the incident and center it on the heart on your beingness.

## 20

# Letting Go of Insistence in Desiring

*If I adore You out of fear of Hell, burn me in Hell.
If I adore You out of desire for Paradise, lock me out of Paradise.
But if I adore You for Yourself alone,
do not deny to me Your Eternal Beauty.*

~ Rabia al Basri

Do your desires drive you, burn you, or awaken you? This question is so profound that it is also the answer. It directly points at what is going on within you. Honestly, tell yourself, "What is my state today with regard to my desires?"

Desires keep arising within us, and we work to fulfill them. Each person is a unique bundle of desires. A unique set of thoughts arise in him to manifest these desires. Thus, the entire world operates because of desires. It is fine as long as our desires drive us, but we need to introspect whether they are burning us within? Let us understand how desires burn us.

Two vessels were filled with water. When the water in the first vessel was placed on the gas stove and started boiling, the second vessel was then placed for heating. A frog was put into each vessel. What was the result? The frog placed in the vessel with boiling water immediately jumped out because its body started to get scalded. The other frog that was placed in the cool water that was being heated kept swimming around. Because the water was getting heated slowly, the frog was getting used to the warmer water. After a while, the water became so hot that the frog started to get scalded, but it could not discern the difference and eventually died.

Our desires are burning us precisely in the same manner. We have got so very used to entertaining them and enduring the suffering caused by them that we fail to realize they are burning us. If we don't become aware of them in time, they will destroy us one day. And, if we become aware, they can awaken us.

For example, if one harbors a desire to complete a task and a guest arrives untimely, he becomes irritated and angry. As soon as he senses a hurdle in fulfilling his desire, his anger burns him. On the other hand, he feels happy when his desire is fulfilled. He then starts harboring a new desire. If that desire doesn't get satisfied, he becomes unhappy. In this way, he gets entangled in the cycle of happiness and sorrow caused by his desires. His desires start burning him, and he gets used to them just like the frog got used to the warm water.

Desires burn him because he doesn't know how to entertain and handle them. When one grooms a pet dog, he ensures to vaccinate it not to harm anyone. Similarly, we should vaccinate ourselves with wisdom so that desires don't burn us and make us sad.

It is not wrong to have desires but desiring a desire is wrong. One harbors a desire that his family members should speak to him politely. Although the desire is seemingly noble, it can burn him if he is not free of desiring the desire.

In spirituality, it is a misunderstanding that one should not harbor any worldly desire. The truth is that desires don't entangle us in the illusory world, but the insistence on gratifying them makes us unhappy. We need to understand that if our desire is as per the divine plan, nature will surely fulfill it. In other words, the attachment to the desire, the insistence on gratifying it should end. As soon as a desire arises, we should be able to say, "If it is according to my divine plan, then let it be fulfilled." Then becoming unhappy for desires and burning due to them will end.

The aim is to reduce the burning due to desires in the seeker's life. As soon as anger or unhappiness arises, he should consciously ask himself, "Which of my desires is being hindered? Can I let go of that desire? Can I enjoy a desire-free state?" By doing this, the desire will help him awaken instead of burning him.

When the seeker takes out some time and observes his desires, he realizes how desires incessantly arise in his mind without his awareness. For example, when there is a power failure, he realizes that he has the desire, "There should be no power failure." When someone rings a doorbell, he realizes that he has the desire, "Now, no one should disturb me." This observation helps him become aware of his subtle desires. He watches how one desire arises and gets fulfilled; then the next one arises; if it is not fulfilled, it causes sorrow. This witnessing of desires and the practice of being in a desire-free state for some time helps him realize the play of desires, and his awareness increases.

Even in the desire-free state, his ultimate desire is getting fulfilled. Meaning, without harboring any desire, he is spontaneously propelled towards bright progress. When he realizes this, he starts leading a life aligned with his true nature.

A mouse desired to become a cat. Obviously, the desire arose out of fear for the cat. Thus, desire arises out of fear. This explains how defilements give birth to inappropriate desires. Then ignorance justifies it, "Yes, this will solve the problem. If I become someone like Bill Gates, this problem will be solved." It seems logically right.

The seeker walking the path to Enlightenment needs to monitor all his desires and check whether they are like that of the mouse. Every person has an inherent pattern, and his desires are based on that pattern. His life is spent in the service of that pattern. He feels it justified as he has developed that formula for safeguarding himself.

Without imbibing the understanding of the Truth, no matter what you achieve in life, you won't be satisfied. Tendencies can never lead you to satisfaction. If you remain in your beingness, you can enjoy satisfaction in any situation. From the outside, you may feel, "This work is unfinished... That task is pending." And yet, there will be a spark in your eyes.

After gaining understanding, you treat those who cater to your desires and those who don't, alike. This is because you clearly know that by not catering to your desires, the other person is actually helping you fulfill your ultimate desire of stabilizing on the Self.

Can there be a more beautiful arrangement than this where you can understand that your wish gets fulfilled without being fulfilled!? Without this understanding, you may have realized that some wishes come true while some don't. Unknowingly, you were fostering wrong desires. They came to light and were removed. After getting the understanding, your wish will always be fulfilled because it is according to the divine will.

## The bright desire

When you are in a mall, at the cinema, at home, in front of the TV, with your neighbor, in the office, or meeting your boss, notice what desires arise within you. You will realize that these are all personalized desires that arise for gratifying the motives of the individual 'I.' They arise to fulfill the demands of the body-mind.

When you meditate, you dwell in your beingness and experience a state of freedom. You wish this state should always remain; you should always experience love, bliss, and peace. This wish is a bright desire. The desire to experience "Who am I?" is a bright desire. There is no personalized ambition in it.

The bright desire gets suppressed amidst other desires. Alertness is necessary to keep the bright desire kindled within. Maya dominates our mind to such an extent that our choices get influenced by the decisions of people around us. "Someone has opened a hotel. Someone else has opened a hospital. Someone else has opened a big gym. I also have to do something." This illusory truth stifles our bright desire. So, be careful. Never let the bright desire get stifled by the illusory truth. Even by listening to the song of a nightingale, one can drown in wonder about the grace that has touched her that she chirps so sweetly. I, too, can sing like her. But if one is lost to the subtler delights of nature, the question of awakening such a desire does not arise.

A seeker should always strengthen his desire to be liberated while his body is alive. Being in the company of people who have the same goal of Enlightenment helps bolster his desire. When he is in the company of the Guru, seeing the Guru boosts his desire for Enlightenment.

Devotee Shabari's divine desire was so strong that Lord Rama would come and meet her. Her feelings, thoughts, speech, and actions were aligned with only one desire—to meet Lord Rama. Her every activity from morning till night was aimed at inviting the Lord. Otherwise, even if one thinks of attaining Enlightenment, he is filled with doubts about it. His speech is filled with arrogance, and his actions serve his selfish motives. When our feelings, thoughts, speech, and actions are aligned, we shift from multidimensional desires to a single bright desire. Only then is liberation possible while the body is alive.

While walking on the path to Enlightenment, when one dwells in the feeling of oneness, immersed in unconditional love and devotion, the desire for Enlightenment automatically ends. Then he remains surrendered in the feeling, "Thy will is alone my will." This is the highest state of acceptance and surrender in which the devotee's desire for Enlightenment also dissolves in divine love with complete surrender. How is the love of Radha and the Gopis for their beloved Lord Krishna? They had no desire for Enlightenment; there was only unselfish and unconditional love. But until such a state is achieved, we need to keep strengthening the bright desire. We need to ensure that we don't lose it in the allure of Maya.

**Action plan**

**1. Fasting with willful neglect**

To break free from the insistence of fulfilling desires, one needs to undertake the practice of desire-fasting with indifference. Here, indifference means an attitude of "Neither yes nor no." Out of habit, the mind may bring up a desire that something should happen, or something should not happen. At such a time, we should consciously evoke a feeling of indifference and say, "If this desire is fulfilled, then so be it. If it does not get fulfilled, then so be it."

For example, suppose you are meditating, and a desire arises, "I was able to meditate deeply yesterday. I should be able to experience the same depth today." You need to witness this desire with indifference by saying, "If deep meditation happens, so be it. If it doesn't happen, then so be it."

Sometimes the seeker feels restless about when he will be freed from the tendency of anger. Why is he still not able to break free from anger despite practicing rigorous sadhana? At that point, bring up a sense of indifference, "If the anger is there, so be it. If it is not there, then so be it." When you perceive it with such indifference, your reaction stops, the restlessness subsides, and a state of stillness arises. No external influence, feeling, or thought can shake you from that state because you are in the state of indifference. In other words, you become indifferent to every desire that arises within you in this state. You live in harmony with nature in the feeling of "Thy will is my will." You will be surprised to see that when you are indifferent to your desires and do not cling to them, your mind becomes empty, and you experience oneness with beingness; you dwell in eternal bliss.

Bear in mind that indifference does not mean doing nothing. It is an attitude of ultimate acceptance. It can also be called the power of indifferent enthusiasm. It helps to act with detachment, where one is passionate about karma but dispassionate about its fruit. If it happens, let it happen, or else let it not happen. Thus, desire-fasting with indifference gets rid of the insistence that desires must be fulfilled.

## 2. Strengthen the bright desire

Strengthen your bright desire during daily chores. For this, shift your attention from mundane desires to the bright desire. Indicate clearly to nature that you earnestly wish for Enlightenment. Put it into words when you pray. Also, express it in writing.

# PART 4

# THE FIVE PILLARS OF ENLIGHTENMENT

A high-rise building can stand erect only when founded on a solid bedrock. If the foundation is weak, then even if the building is constructed, it can collapse at the slightest of tremors.

This is true for the foundation of Enlightenment too. There are five aspects that form the pillars for Enlightenment. It is vital to properly understand these aspects and integrate them into your life to attain Enlightenment.

In this part, we shall understand these five pillars and work towards making them the very fiber of the fabric of our life.

## 21

# Pure Mind
## The First Pillar

*There is no need to travel anyplace on pilgrimage.
The greatest and most sacred of shrines is your mind,
which has to be primarily cleansed and sanctified.*

~ Adi Shankaracharya

A clear sky is necessary to get a good glimpse of the moon. Even a single cloud can shroud it. Similarly, a pure mind is essential to experience Enlightenment. Otherwise, even a trivial defilement can distract and dissuade the seeker from the state of Enlightenment.

The human mind can be broadly classified into two facets: the contrast mind and the intuitive mind. The intuitive mind functions spontaneously. However, the contrast mind resorts to comparison, deceit, judgment, logic, and imagination. It is contaminated by the impurities of false beliefs and faulty impressions. No matter how hard one tries to control this mind, the effort proves to be in vain.

When one walks on the path to Enlightenment, one understands the subtler aspects of the mind. He witnesses the play of the contrast mind – how it engages in constant comparison, how it entangles him and hinders the right understanding and attainment of Truth.

In the previous part, we have seen how the contrast mind can align with the Self, taste true bliss, become absorbed in divine devotion, and prepare to surrender and support in attaining Enlightenment.

The mind surrenders only when it is pure. The seeker must have a pure and open mind to tread on the path to Enlightenment. The mind is rendered impure by the scathing serpent of hatred, the haughty camel of ego, the wily fox of greed, and the scary demon of fear. When the filth of these defilements is removed from the mind, it becomes pure. When the mind is as honest and sincere like an innocent child, it is said to be a pure mind.

How do we feel in the company of little children? Don't we experience the spark of clarity and simplicity? Our stress reduces and we feel pleasant in the company of children. What special energy do children radiate? It is the energy of purity and innocence! When the seeker becomes a child again, in other words, when his mind becomes honest and unblemished, then the state of Enlightenment unfolds.

Since ancient times, the purity of mind has been given utmost importance in the journey to Enlightenment. Maharishi Patanjali preached the path of Ashtanga Yoga to attain Enlightenment. Of those eight limbs of yoga, the first two emphasize purifying the mind. The five *Yamas* (abstinences) and five *Niyamas* (observances) have been prescribed for this. The Buddha also preached the five precepts of Panchsheel to purify the mind. A pure mind is a prerequisite for entering the shrine of Enlightenment. Every religion has emphasized the purity of mind.

There are ample examples where God manifested Himself to His innocent, loving, sinless devotees. Lord Krishna turned down the cunning and arrogant Duryodhana's invitation to the royal feast. Instead, he accompanied the righteous devotee Vidura to a simple holy meal. Lord Rama himself walked into devotee Shabari's hermitage and ended her years of ardent yearning by granting her Enlightenment. These examples highlight the significance of a pure mind.

The exceptional powers of the mind are revealed to a seeker treading the path to Enlightenment. He also attains many occult powers (*siddhis*) during meditation. Consider them a milestone in the journey to Enlightenment and move on. Otherwise, if one attains these powers with an impure mind, his chances of getting entangled in them increase manifold. Therefore, in ancient times, sages used to assess the seeker's merit before imparting wisdom. The seeker would render service by staying in the hermitage for a few years. When the Guru was convinced that the seeker's mind had become pure, his big tendencies had vanished, and now he won't misuse the knowledge; moreover, he would use the powers for the welfare of all, then and only then would the Guru impart wisdom to him. Many sages had set out for Enlightenment but deviated from the path due to impure mind and became arrogant after attaining powers.

Ravana was a great devotee of Lord Shiva. He worshipped the Lord with great reverence. But after attaining powers, his ego inflated. The world knows how an impure mind led to his grave downfall. On the other hand, Vibhishana's pure mind led him to the sacred company of Lord Rama.

When one serves selflessly for the wellbeing of all, when he progresses from personal aspirations to an impersonal selfless goal, his mind starts getting purified. In ancient times, when people used to render selfless service by staying in the hermitage, they would rise beyond their selfish interests and develop an impersonal perspective.

There is the story of the enlightened King Janaka, who was being escorted to heaven. When his entourage took a detour through hell on the way, he was agonized at seeing the inhabitants of hell in intense pain and suffering. Overwhelmed with compassion, a heartfelt prayer arose from within him for their liberation. He prayed, "May all the merits that I've attained on Earth through my sadhana be offered for the healing and betterment of these ailing beings."

King Janaka's immense power of righteousness washed away the sins of all beings. All those inhabitants were freed from their painful hell. What a pure and unblemished mind this is! Every seeker should draw inspiration from King Janaka for how compassionately he offered his lifelong penance for universal wellbeing.

The intention of universal wellbeing purifies our mind. When we offer our every effort towards Enlightenment, be it listening to the

Truth, meditation, praying, or serving for universal wellbeing, it enhances our purity of mind.

The pillar of a pure mind can be strengthened with meditation and prayer.

## 1. Practice of Meditation

Meditation, in essence, is the quality of the Self-witnesser, also known as God, Allah, or Consciousness. The main goal of meditation is to experience the omnipresent Self that transcends the body, mind, and intellect, where only undivided oneness prevails. During meditation, the seeker clearly observes the defilements, tendencies, and impurities of his mind in a detached manner. Such observation helps in getting rid of them easily. The more his mind revels being in the experience of the Self, the more it gets cleansed by itself.

Angulimal used to loot and kill people regularly. Just imagine how much his mind was filled with hatred! Yet even such an impure mind became purified when the Buddha graced him by bestowing him the practice of meditation.

Daily meditation with understanding helps the seeker to remain aware during his routine activities. It safeguards him from the tendencies of his mind. Therefore, it is necessary to dwell in meditation for some time every day. It purifies the mind and leads one closer to Enlightenment.

## 2. Prayer

We all have been bestowed with the wondrous tool of prayer for purifying the mind. Prayer means asking for something. And usually, we ask for something from someone superior to us. The feeling of prayer absorbs our mind in a state of surrender, devotion, and void of ego. In this state, we are closer to our pure nature. The purer the mind becomes, the closer we move to Enlightenment.

Our prayer changes according to our state of mind. Initially, we pray for material pleasures, comforts, and conveniences. We pray for our wellbeing and that of our family. Gradually, we understand that the same consciousness pervades all. Our wellbeing lies in the wellbeing of all. Then our prayer changes. We pray for universal wellbeing. Thus, our subconscious mind gets purified, which helps in attaining Enlightenment.

Faith and feeling form the soul of prayer. Words are not as important in prayer as feelings are because feelings yield results, not words. Similarly, we get evidence for whatever we believe. If we believe that Enlightenment is indeed possible, we will certainly experience it. If we believe that it is difficult, it is not possible in this lifetime, then it becomes impossible.

The power of prayer is unfathomable! For instance -

When one prays for a bright future, he doesn't realize that with this prayer, he can actually be free from both the burden of the past and the worries of the future at a time!

When one prays for a cure of his illness, he doesn't know that he can be liberated from the cycle of birth and death by the power of prayer!

When one prays to score well in her exams, to gain knowledge of everything, she forgets that she could have discovered the secrets of the universe with true prayer!

When one prays to attain Enlightenment, she does not realize that when her false 'I' falls, she will become instrumental for the liberation of thousands of people.

This is the power and glory of prayer. A mind purified by prayer attains the pinnacle of the inner world; it is welcomed in the court of God. Let us pray from the heart for Enlightenment.

*"Dear God! I don't know what Enlightenment is,*

*I can't imagine it either,*

*but I am expressing my feelings to you through words!*

*May I be blessed with the ultimate Truth, the state of Enlightenment*

*that has been glorified by the great masters!*

*Gratitude!"*

## 22

# Karma Without Bondage
## The Second Pillar

*If only you can abide in pure consciousness,
knowing yourself beyond the body,
then in this very moment,
you'll be in bliss, peace, and freedom from bondage.*

~ Sage Ashtavakra

It is often said, "Freedom from the bondage of karma is Enlightenment." The subject of karmic bondage has been discussed so extensively in spirituality that one hesitates to perform any karma, although human birth and karma are deeply intertwined. No one can live without performing karma. Our very existence on Earth is a declaration of karma. Even if we choose not to act, the choice of inaction is also a form of karma.

Karma performed with the right understanding can open the door to Enlightenment; otherwise, it can create more bondage. Hence, seekers seeking to attain Enlightenment should first acquire the understanding that will render their karma the basis for Enlightenment.

Let us understand which karma leads to bondage and which one to Enlightenment.

## 1. Reactive karma causes bondage

Most people consider performing their daily tasks as karma. However, it is not karma; it is reactive karma. If you reflect on this, you will find that you act under the influence of external events. For example, if someone abuses you, you retaliate. If the other person doesn't abuse you, you won't abuse him either. This means, whether you abuse or not depends on the other person's action. The other person holds the reins of your karma.

Someone appreciates you, and you admire him too. Otherwise, you wouldn't have complimented him. These are all reactive actions. Whether you appreciate or accuse, your reaction creates a subtle thread and binds you to that person. Consider your age and how many people you have connected with so far? What a vast, invisible web of karmic bondage you have woven around you! It pulls you in from all sides and makes you feel bounded.

So, what's the way out? Perform karma intuitively, not as a reaction. Make sure to consistently act with awareness. For this, keep asking yourself, "Am I acting intuitively or as a reaction to others' behavior? Why did I help someone? Was it because he appreciated me or because it was the right thing to do?" The torch of understanding should guide us, not the behavior of others. This is the first step to strengthen the pillar of karma.

## 2. The feeling behind karma causes either bondage or liberation

Most people get entangled in the superficial tangible form of karma. They consider only speech and actions to be karma and ignore their feelings. Karma actually comprises both action and feeling. Although your actions may outwardly seem noble, if your feelings are of greed, selfishness, and ego, then such actions also bind you. On the other hand, a simple act done with a benevolent feeling doesn't create any bondage.

For example, two women have guests at home. The first one cooks a delicious meal thinking, "Today, they have to appreciate my expertise in cooking," or "Hey! I'm overloaded. Guests have no sense of time." Such feelings create bondage, even if she cooks a delicious meal and feeds them with outward hospitality. On the other hand, the other lady cheerfully welcomes the guests. She cooks a simple and healthy meal with the sentiment, "May this meal bring health and peace to the guests! I have got the opportunity to serve them." Such a feeling liberates her from all bondage, even if she doesn't put up an impressive act of hospitality.

In one context, a judge sentences a criminal to death, and the executioner hangs him. In another context, someone commits murder for revenge. Though someone is being killed in both the contexts, there is a big difference. The judge and executioner are doing their duty to society, while the murderer is filled with anger and hatred.

Feelings harbored while performing karma play an important role in attaining Enlightenment. A seeker should be aware of his feelings while dealing with the world.

### 3. Non-doership releases bondage

One often shies away from performing karma out of fear of bondage. But such a non-doership is mere inaction. Instead, he needs to free himself from the feeling of doership while performing karma. In other words, if he gets rid of the ignorance of "I am doing the action," then his actions won't create bondage. Everyone can attain the state of non-doership in this very life. Those who aspire for Enlightenment must not rest until they attain the state of non-doership.

For this, a seeker should surrender every small action to God. For example, if you help someone, remind yourself, "God alone is the doer of this karma." When you return from shopping, remember, "God has performed the act of shopping." God, or the fundamental essence, is functioning through all bodies. Remember this truth while performing every action and surrender it to God. This feeling of surrender will lead to the state of non-doership and strengthen the pillar of karma.

Two people perform the karma of charity for the wellbeing of people. But the first person donates with the feeling, "I have donated." So, even his noble karma creates bondage for him. He forgets that God is making his body instrumental for performing that karma. Although his karma is pious, it is still a golden handcuff that causes bondage. The other person understands the essence of non-doership. Therefore, he surrenders every karma to God. He would say, "It is due to God that this body is being given the thought of charity. Gratitude to God for making this body instrumental for the Divine will!"

## 4. Desire-less karma releases bondage

When karma is performed without clinging to its fruit, it is called "Desire-less karma." Such karma helps in attaining Enlightenment. Otherwise, it invites bondage. Reflect on each of your actions: What is the intention behind it? Do you work hard in the office to get promoted? Do you cook delicious food to please your family? Do you provide higher education to your children so that they will support you when you are aged?

When a true, honest artist paints a picture, or a musician plays with joy, do they expect recognition and fame in return? No, they will say, "I am enjoying this creative expression so much that I don't need anything other than this." A seeker treading the path to Enlightenment should have such an attitude.

The seeker should discharge his worldly duties with the understanding that everything is a part of the spontaneous happening. Even the fruit of actions will unfold as a part of the spontaneous happening, so don't get caught in it. The joy he experiences while meditating, serving for the wellbeing of people, or participating in a spiritual discourse is a fruit in itself! The desire for any other gain will trap him in bondage. Karma performed with a pure feeling certainly bears the highest fruit. But we should not act in the hope of a fixed fruit.

Many enlightened saints performed the karma of preaching the Truth. We all know Saint Kabir's *Dohe*, Saint Tukaram's *Abhanga*, Saint Meera's *Bhajans*, the Buddha's Preaching. They all performed selfless desire-free karma. They never placed a condition, "The disciples must obey what I preach." They were brimming with such boundless love, unconditional joy, and wisdom that karma intuitively happened through them.

## 5. Karma, backed by wisdom, releases bondage

The greatest karma is to attain understanding which helps complete the journey to Enlightenment. Regularly listening to discourses on the Truth, reading Truth literature, meditation, and chanting help deepen understanding. Then the seeker experientially knows: Who is performing karma through all the bodies? Who is lost in a stupor? Who has to be aware? It is only in the light of awareness that all actions dissolve in the flame of wisdom. Then there is neither the doer nor the experiencer. Everything happens naturally and spontaneously. This is the state of Enlightenment!

For performing karma backed by wisdom, develop the habit of dwelling in your beingness before every action. It helps shed all your labels, perspectives, wrong beliefs, and assumptions. Whatever thoughts, advice, decisions emerge after that prove to be pure, worthy, supreme, and perfect. Such actions work for the wellbeing of all. The habit of dwelling in beingness before every action strengthens the pillar of karma and opens the door to Enlightenment.

## 23

# Nectar of Devotion
## The Third Pillar

*The moon will perish, and so will the sun;*
*The earth will perish, and so will the skies;*
*The wind will vanish and so too will water;*
*All that will remain is that Imperishable One!*

~ Saint Meera

As long as devotion does not awaken, one does not fancy it; but once it has awakened, nothing else seems worthwhile! This is the glory of devotion. When divine devotion awakens and you experience its sweetness, all the charm of the world fades before it. Enlightenment cannot be beyond the reach of a true devotee. Hence, it is said that devotion is complete in itself.

The third and pivotal pillar of Enlightenment is devotion. Devotion is God's gift to man, which has the power to dissolve the ego. Karma, wisdom, and meditation are important aspects leading to Enlightenment, but they attain completeness only when they are accompanied by devotion. While wisdom is a prequisite for attaining Enlightenment, devotion is essential to retain that state. Devotion reminds us from time to time that wisdom should not be used to satisfy the ego but to be free from all tendencies.

The relationship between a devotee and God is like a moth to a flame. When the flame is kindled, the moth rushes to it by itself. The moth is the devotee in love of the flame. Wherever it may be, it is drawn towards the flame. Despite knowing that it will lose its existence by getting close to the flame, it embraces the flame by casting away all care.

The moth is not concerned about anything other than the flame. Similarly, the devotee does not care about anything other than God. Otherwise, one is so overwhelmed with worldly worries that he rarely remembers about Enlightenment. But, once it loses itself in devout love for the flame, it does not bother to approach it despite knowing that it will meet its end.

Being surrendered in devotion, some exceptional wonders unfold in the world of lovers that others cannot comprehend. Saint Meera happily drank the poison; Saint Tukaram remained firm in devotion even when his abhangas were thrown in the river; Saint Dnyaneshwar composed the Dnyaneshwari, despite being oppressed by the society. Such expression is possible only in devotion!

Just as the moth is prepared to die in love, a true devotee completely surrenders and is prepared to drown his individuality in the ocean of devotion.

You use glass for drinking water. But if the glass itself causes entanglement, then better use a glass made of ice so that you drink the glass itself while you drink the water. In other words, the glass that serves as a medium for drinking water also eventually dissolves.

Similarly, fill the glass of your body with so much devotion that it doesn't cause any entanglement. You will not even realize when the individual ego gradually dissolved in devotion, leading to Enlightenment! This is the zenith of devotion.

Saint Kabir, Saint Meera, Saint Tukaram, and Saint Eknath are examples of devotees who lost themselves in devotion and became one with devotion! The way devotees like Sudama and Prahlad demonstrated devotion in their life is also inspiring for all. Their conviction kindles the supreme quest within us.

Prahlad was an exceptional devotee. His father Hiranyakashyapa was a vicious king. He arrogantly declared himself to be the almighty. Despite the king's numerous attempts, Prahlad didn't stop worshipping God. Finally, one day, he threatened Prahlad to throw him off the mountain. But even his threats couldn't deter Prahlad from his devotion. He stood firm in his faith. He was thrown off the mountain, but he remained unhurt!

If someone abuses you and threatens to throw you off the mountain, and you also abuse and curse him in return, it means you have already rolled down the mountain of awareness even before he pushes you!

Prahlad welcomed every trouble as the grace of God. He lived life with the faith, "Thy Will is my will." He had unwavering faith in God. Hence, even after being thrown from the mountain, he softly landed in the lap of God. This is possible only in devotion!

What spiritual power Jesus had! He could easily forgive the perpetrators even when he was being crucified. Even in his last moments, he prayed, "Father, forgive them, for they do not know what they are doing." Jesus could say this because he was not concerned about anyone other than the all-pervading One! This is the supreme devotion, where the devotee surrenders to the will of the Lord.

A true devotee blissfully witnesses the trials of life and enjoys how everything unfolds as a part of the divine happening. Absorbed in devotion, he considers pain and pleasure as the two aspects of the same bliss. Sudama could live happily amid extreme poverty and scarcity with such supreme devotion. Despite living on crumbs with his family for years, he never complained to God. He never doubted devotion. If a monk arrived during his mealtime, he would feed the monk and remain hungry. He lived by the wisdom and instructions of the Guru. His spiritual strength evolved, and his devotion remained unwavering in all odds. This is the grace that devotion bestows in the life of the devotee!

The devotee never prays for worldly pleasures. Surrendered in devotion, he lives with a feeling of "Thy will is my will." An intense prayer arises within him, "Dear God, May Your sweet remembrance immerse me in the ocean of Your Being. May the utterance of Your Name flood me with tears."

Grope within yourself and check, "Does such deep longing, such intense prayer arise within me? What level of devotion have I attained?" A seeker should leave no stone unturned in fostering his devotion. Devotion is complete in itself. Because, once devotion is awakened, all other possibilities begin to un-fold naturally.

A few steps with awareness can help awaken devotion.

1. The first step to deepen your devotion is to adore divine qualities. It is the law of nature, "You become what you describe." Listening to the stories about devotees and deeply contemplating their qualities awakens the essence of devotion within us. Ponder, "What made these devotees choose the One above all? What passion did they have?"

2. A seeker should always ensure that his devotion weighs more than his tendencies. Once the ratio of tendencies and devotion becomes 49:51, you will experience that the obstacles of tendencies are gradually getting removed from the spiritual path, and devotion is deepening. Even if tendencies emerge, devotion will nip them in the bud.

A devotee who seeks Enlightenment leaves no stone unturned. The slightest wavering of devotion or even the slightest separation from God is painful to him. He wipes it off immediately with awareness.

3. A seeker should always be in the company of those who have given the highest priority to devotion and strived for divine devotion. Join them in reading, contemplation, listening to the Truth, chanting, devotional veneration, and meditation, and the stream of devotion will automatically flow. The company of Truth will always inspire, motivate, and awaken faith within you.

4. Develop an eye of equanimity to raise devotion. Instead of judging the shortcomings in others, watch them with evenness. Don't discriminate between people based on color, race, appearance, religion, rank, or position. A devotee perceives the same consciousness in all beings. Saint Namdev had this vision due to

which he could see Lord Vitthala even in a dog! When the dog ran away with his bread, he ran after the dog to apply butter so that his Lord would not have to eat dry bread!

5. When devotion is associated with rituals, people mistake listening to mythical stories, ritualistic worship, and fasting as devotion. However, it only inflates the ego instead of devotion. So, be aware not to serve the ego. Once the ego vanishes, true devotion awakens.

When divine devotion awakens, the ego of individuality dissolves. Then, not just the 'I', but its whole family of beliefs and notions is surrendered. It means all labels attached to 'I,' all imaginations, all judgments are surrendered. When the whole family is surrendered, there remains no hindrance from labels that could otherwise have frightened, allured, or made you serve the ego. On attaining true devotion, yogis do not deviate from yoga, meditators do not deviate from meditation, and the wise do not grieve. When devotion gets associated with yoga, meditation and wisdom, then only Enlightenment remains.

Devotion has been glorified so much on the path to Enlightenment because it balances all the paths like chanting, penance, tantra, karma, meditation, and wisdom.

If you eat ice-cream in a cone, what is the role of the cone in it? It holds the ice-cream and doesn't let it fall. Also, the cone has some ingredients that complement and help digest the ice-cream.

Devotion serves the same purpose as the ice-cream cone on the path to Enlightenment. Initially, the seeker aims for equanimity. Gradually, he becomes mature, disciplined, righteous, simple, pure, and equanimous. But, soon, his life becomes mechanical and tasteless. The sweetness of life is lost. He doesn't find that energy to go further beyond equanimity into the transcendental attribute-less state. It has often been observed that seekers start the reverse journey on reaching the milestone of equanimity. Here comes the role of devotion! Devotion saves the seeker. The sweetness of devotion inspires the seeker to move further ahead. Devotion is the secret of consistent sadhana for Enlightenment.

## The Height of Devotion

The height of devotion is where devotion attains the pinnacle, and the pinnacle also attains the highest form of devotion. This supreme state of devotion was attained by Saint Meera, where she was blessed with Krishna consciousness, and consciousness was also graced by the devotion of Meera! Meera attained Enlightenment, and Enlightenment attained Meera! Even Enlightenment was graced with Meera's devotion!

May such a bright flame of divine devotion be kindled in the heart of every devotee before which everything else will fade away. He will only care about that "flame" and lose himself in it!

## 24

# Self-Introspection
## The Fourth Pillar

*Facts are many, but the truth is one.*

~ Rabindranath Tagore

Self-introspection is an essential milestone on the journey to Enlightenment. Here, self-introspection has a dual meaning—witnessing the body-mind and knowing the Self. We often mistake introspection of the body-mind as knowing the Self. We consider witnessing our body-mind as the glimpse of Self. But the two are entirely different.

When we meditate on the Self, our true nature, this Self-remembrance is Self-realization. And when we honestly witness our body, mind, and intellect with detachment, it is self-introspection. Both are equally important as their confluence helps to stabilize on the Self. During the combined practice of body-mind introspection and Self-witnessing, we gain the conviction of our true nature as the untouched immaculate Self beyond the body-mind.

The quality of contemplating on the Self helps us dive deeper into meditation. The inner silence experienced in deep meditation remains unaffected regardless of any situation. With the practice of meditating on the Self and the habit of body-mind introspection, we get to know a great deal about ourselves.

Usually, we are curious to know about others more than ourselves! Instead of inquiring into ourselves, we keep inquiring about the world, "What's happening around? Who has come to the neighbor's house? When does he go? Where does he go? What outfit does he wear? What's the latest news in the country?" We rarely pay heed to, "What's going on within me? What is the nature of my body-mind mechanism?"

When we learn the art of introspecting our body-mind, we understand the subtle aspects of our mind. With the help of the weapon of our mind, we can either realize our true nature, or drift away from the Truth. The mind diverts us away from the Self by weaving new stories, by getting caught up in the allure of Maya, or by engaging in comparison. Self-introspection is the first step by which we come to know the play of our mind as it is. Once the mind is conquered through introspection and immersed in devotion, it helps us attain Enlightenment.

While introspecting the mind, we witness the various states of our mind and the thoughts that arise. We witness negative, positive, or neutral thoughts arising in every incident. While introspecting the body, we understand whether our body is lazy, hyperactive, or balanced. We witness the kind of emotions that arise most often in our body-mind, like fear, hatred, arrogance, anger, jealousy, guilt, greed, joy, wonder, love, kindness, compassion, etc. We also observe how the mind changes when the senses assail us.

By detaching from the body-mind, we can clearly witness the mind's tendencies, patterns, and habits. We observe how our mind has the habit of judging others, comparing, being unhappy, blaming others, avoiding situations, not living in the present, and wandering in the past and the future. We witness the rise and fall of our ego in various situations. We become aware of the patterns and tendencies that hinder our journey to Enlightenment.

When we imbibe the habit of contemplation, we can grasp even the slightest signals of nature. Actually, the entire universe is guiding us towards Enlightenment, provided we are receptive and understand its indications. Every situation, every person we meet, the scenes we encounter, everything is guiding us to raise our level of awareness. But due to lack of contemplation, we fail to understand these indications. For example, if we get fired, we think, "The boss is ill-tempered," or "Someone must have turned him against me," or "This company is worthless, running at a loss," etc. In contrast, the situation indicates the ever-changing nature of life. If we are able to catch the right cue, we will calmly look for the next job and put ourselves on the path to Enlightenment.

Many saints attained the pinnacle of spiritual growth through the art of contemplation. They learned a lot by deeply contemplating on birds, animals, insects, and trees around them. They believed that everyone could learn something from every living and non-living being.

If we are not used to introspecting with awareness, we can easily get caught up in the lure of occult powers. We can drift off the spiritual path after achieving such powers. We can get entangled in the illusory attractions of Maya and put our mission on Earth at stake. Having attained occult powers, we don't realize when our ego gets inflated, and we crave fame and greatness. Therefore, it is important to introspect from time to time. Before the dust of illusion settles, wipe it off with introspection!

If we believe that mere chanting of the Guru mantra will help us attain Enlightenment, it's an illusion. Bear in mind that this may be the mind's trick to refrain from honestly introspecting and avoid facing our inner truth. But without introspection, it is difficult to be free from the illusory trap of Maya.

The ego (separate individuality) always tries to safeguard itself. It causes delusion so that it survives and thrives forever. Introspection helps to capture this play of the ego. Once its tendencies, patterns, and habits come to light, there is a possibility of breaking free from them. Hence, the first important step is to bring them in the light of your awareness, after which they begin to weaken.

The biggest advantage of the habit of introspection is that it helps us realize our shortcomings immediately, reflect on them, and rectify them. This reduces the risk of deviating from the path to Enlightenment. As soon as we begin to fall, we rise again. The time taken to realize and correct the mistake gradually decreases. Increased awareness prevents committing further mistakes. In other words, the habit of introspection sets the pace for achieving the goal of Enlightenment.

For introspection, we can follow the steps given below:

**Be your own detective**

We need to become our own detective. Investigate every negative thought and feeling that arises in our mind, just as a detective interrogates an accused and unearths the truth. Be careful not to act reactively.

For example, suppose you help a friend but deny help to others. You need to ask yourself why you indulged in such discriminatory behavior. Is it because the first friend always complies with you and never has a conflict with you, or because the other person didn't help you in times of your need?

Learn to bust your mind in this manner. Bring to light all the subtle aspects of the mind. Be attentive to all your activities and honestly inquire from time to time, "Is this path leading me to spiritual growth? Am I striving to be recognized as someone 'special?' Do I feel like stopping at this juncture of fame? Am I progressing to the next level of awareness?"

**Introspect Daily**

Make a habit of noting down the incidents that occurred during the day before going to bed in a journal. Contemplate in writing, "How did I spend the day? Do the actions that I have taken help me break free from bondage and lead me to Enlightenment, or do they entangle me and divert me from the path to Enlightenment? What incidents happened, and how did the mind chatter? What was the basis of decisions taken during the day?" Witness their futility too. The whole picture becomes clear after writing. Once the mind is penned on paper, it is easy to come up with the next action plan.

A pot fills drop by drop. Similarly, the pot of understanding fills with the practice of meditation, contemplation, listening to the Truth, and serving selflessly for some time every day. This propels us towards Enlightenment.

We need to read the biographies of the great souls who have attained Enlightenment. Get a sense of the passion that drove them to complete their journey. They didn't deviate from their goal even for a moment. Their every response was a step towards their goal. They were always aware of the attacks of the illusory world. We should also strive to achieve that level of awareness.

# 25

# Thirst and Grace
## The Fifth Pillar

*May all praise and venerate the True Guru,*
*who has led us to the treasure of the divine devotion.*

~ Guru Gobind Singh Ji

Congratulations! You have reached the final milestone in unfolding the journey to Enlightenment. We have understood that this is an inner journey to attain the highest understanding. As we break free from the beliefs, tendencies, desires, and misunderstandings arising from the ego, we can open the door to Enlightenment.

Now, let us understand the pillar that serves as the foundation for all the other pillars. It is the pillar of "Thirst for Truth" and "Grace of the Guru."

Just as we turn the ignition key to start a car, the thirst for Truth acts as a key to ignite the quest for Truth within us. As our thirst intensifies, incidents occur accordingly. The Guru enters our life, we read Truth literature, join the company of truth-seekers, and so on. Nature helps us in every possible way.

Ask the hungry man the value of food and the thirsty man the value of water! They take great pains to seek food and water without any prodding from anyone. Hunger and thirst compel them to do so. In other words, the more intense the hunger or thirst, the greater their effortless effort. They don't have to struggle to put in the effort. Likewise, the longing for Enlightenment transforms our effort not just into effortless effort but into loving effort.

An artist instinctively loses himself in creating incredible works of art regardless of hunger and thirst. Others may feel how hard he is working for hours together without rest. But, if you ask the artist, he will say, "Art is my life! Art flows in my veins. It is an effortless effort for me."

There was a woman who yearned to understand the truth of life. She wanted to renounce the world and become a nun. However, her family did not allow her to pursue this path. They got her married. One day, she opened her heart to her husband, "I wish to be a nun from the bottom of my heart. Will you allow me?" Her husband said, "Yes, I will allow you only after bearing three children." He considered that after having children, she would forget about her religious passion out of affection for her children. But it was not so!

After bearing three children, she stuck to her resolve of becoming a nun. She went to a church and expressed her desire to the pastor. But the pastor refused. When she asked for the reason, he explained, "You are beautiful. Your beauty could possibly be a hindrance to the spiritual practice of the other seekers." Hearing this, she returned home without saying anything to the pastor. The next day she went to him with a burnt face! The father was shocked. She said, "I have burnt my beauty. Now, surely there must be no problem to take me in your fold!"

Just imagine how intense her thirst for Truth was, that made her sacrifice her beauty so easily. We all know how dearly a woman loves her children and her beauty. Such a sacrifice is possible only in supreme thirst.

As the thirst for Truth intensifies, the need for willpower reduces. In the beginning, we have to force ourselves to sit in meditation, listen to the Truth, introspect, and contemplate. Later, the thirst for true bliss becomes so intense that we wish to dwell in beingness forever.

A seeker longing for Enlightenment prays to God, "You have given me the will; you alone will liberate me." This prayer shows that the devotee has a thirst for liberation and the faith that if the desire is given, liberation will be surely granted. Such faith evolves only when the seeker works on himself internally. This means that when there is a thirst for Truth, a readiness to strive out of love, faith in the Guru and Nature, then the grace of God is showered.

With this very faith, Saint Meera could drink poison in the name of Lord Krishna. Such intense faith manifests miracles! Meera had intensely worked within herself to develop such a bright faith within. She had immense devotion towards Lord Krishna and had completely surrendered her ego to Him. Intense thirst makes this happen automatically. Be it Saint Kabir, Saint Ravidas, Sri Ramkrishna Paramhansa, or Adi Guru Shankaracharya, they all had an uncompromising thirst for Truth, loving effort, and infallible faith which bestowed upon them the grace of Enlightenment.

Now, the question is how to deepen the thirst? It's easy! The more time we spend in the company of Truth, the deeper our thirst for Truth becomes. The thirst deepens by listening to the Truth, praying, contemplating, reading scriptures, and being in meditation. And, when the thirst deepens, meditation and prayer happen effortlessly. Thus, it begins the cycle of thirst, loving effort, and bright transformation. The thirst for Enlightenment even deepens in the company of devotees. Therefore, we should heartily pray to God, "May my resolve to attain Enlightenment gather strength! May the divine grace shower on me!"

When we contemplate on grace, we realize that even the bright desire for Enlightenment arises only due to grace. It is indeed a grace to have the right guru in our life. It is also a grace to listen to Truth and to read this book till the end!

And what can be the greater grace than being blessed with the refuge of the Guru! The possibility of being established in the ultimate

Truth unfolds only in the company of the Guru. Seeking refuge in the Guru opens the door to Enlightenment!

Guru means the Enlightened Lamp, the manifest form of God! There are also certain scriptures that are revered as the Guru. Nevertheless, the significance of a living guru is unmatched because a living guru guides us according to our innate nature and tendencies.

The Guru is like a potter, who knows when to shape the earthen pot from outside, when to heat it in the furnace and when to touch it gently from within, to avoid breaking. When a disciple obeys the instructions of the Guru with utmost faith and submission, and attains the destination, his heart is filled with feelings of profound gratitude! Then, these lines of Saint Kabir echo his sentiments -

*Knowledge doesn't blossom without the Guru;*

*Enlightenment isn't attained without the Guru.*

*Truth remains unrevealed without the Guru;*

*Sins aren't washed without the Guru.*

♦ ♦ ♦

---

You can mail your opinion or feedback on this book to: books.feedback@tejgyan.org

## About Sirshree

Sirshree's spiritual quest, which began during his childhood, led him on a journey through various schools of philosophy and meditation practices. He studied a wide range of literature on mind science and spirituality. After a long period of deep contemplation on the truth of life, his quest culminated in attaining the ultimate truth.

Sirshree espouses, "All spiritual paths that lead to the truth begin differently but culminate at the same point – Understanding. This understanding is complete in itself. Listening to this understanding is enough to attain the Truth." Over the last two decades, he has dedicated his life to raise mass consciousness.

Sirshree has delivered more than 4000 discourses that throw light on this understanding. He has designed a system for wisdom, which makes it accessible to all. This system has inspired people from all walks of life to progress on their journey of the Truth. Thousands of seekers join in a virtual prayer for World Peace and Global Healing daily at 9:09 am and 9:09 pm.

# About Tej Gyan Foundation

Tej Gyan Foundation is a non-profit organization founded on the teachings of Sirshree. The Foundation disseminates Tejgyan – the wisdom that guides one from self-development to Self-realization, leading towards Self-stabilization.

The Foundation's system for imparting wisdom has been assessed by international quality auditors and accredited with the ISO 9001:2015 certification. This wisdom has been presented in a simple, systematic, and practically applicable form that makes it accessible to people from all walks of life, regardless of religion, caste, social strata, country, or belief system.

The Foundation has centers in more than 400 cities and towns across India and other countries. The mission of Tej Gyan Foundation is to create a highly evolved society by leading seekers from negative thoughts to positive thoughts and further, from positive thoughts to Happy thoughts. A 'Happy thought' is the auspicious thought of being free from all thoughts, leading to the state of supreme bliss beyond thoughts.

If you seek such wisdom that leads you beyond mere knowledge, dissolves all problems, frees you from all limiting beliefs, reveals the true nature of divinity, and establishes you in the ultimate truth, then it is time to discover Tejgyan; it is time to rise above the mundane knowledge of words and experience Tejgyan!

# The MahaAasmani Magic of Awakening Retreat

## Self-development to Self-realization towards Self-stabilization

Do you wish to experience unconditional happiness that is not dependent on any reason? Happiness that is permanent and only increases with time? Do you wish to experience love, peace, self-belief, harmony in relationships, prosperity, and true contentment? Do you wish to progress in all facets of your life, viz. physical, mental, social, financial, and spiritual?

If you seek answers to these questions and are thirsty for the ultimate truth, then you are welcome to participate in the MahaAasmani Magic of Awakening retreat organized by Tej Gyan Foundation. This is the Foundation's flagship retreat based on the teachings of Sirshree.

**The purpose of this retreat**

The purpose of this retreat is that every human being should:

- Discover the answer to "Who am I" and "Why am I?" through direct experience and be established in ultimate bliss.

- Learn the art of living in the present, free from the burden of the past and the anxiety of the future.

- Acquire practical tools to help quieten the chattering mind and dissolve problems.

- Discover missing links in the practices of Meditation (*Dhyana*), Action (*Karma*), Wisdom (*Gyana*), and Devotion (*Bhakti*).

# About Books by Sirshree

Sirshree's published work includes more than 150 book titles, some of which have been translated into more than 10 languages. His literature provides a profound reading on various topics of practical living and unravels the missing links in karma, wisdom, devotion, meditation, and consciousness.

His books have been published by leading publishing houses like Penguin, Hay House, Bloomsbury, Wisdom Tree, Jaico, etc. "The Source" book series, authored by Sirshree, has sold over 10 million copies. Various luminaries and celebrities like His Holiness the Dalai Lama, publishers Mr. Reid Tracy, Ms. Tami Simon and Yoga Master Dr. B. K. S. Iyengar have released Sirshree's books and lauded his work.

**The Source**
Attain Both, Inner Peace
and Worldly success

**Awaken the Power of Faith**
Discover the 7 Principles of the
Highest Power of the Universe

To order books authored by Sirshree, login to:
www.gethappythoughts.org
For further details, call: +91 9011013210

## SELECT BOOKS AUTHORED BY SIRSHREE

   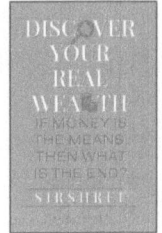

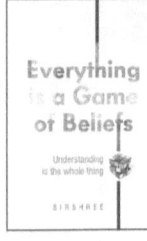   

To order these and other books authored by Sirshree
Visit **www.gethappythoughts.org**

# Tej Gyan Foundation – Contact details

**Registered Office:**
Happy Thoughts Building, Vikrant Complex, Near Tapovan Mandir, Pimpri, Pune 411017, INDIA. Contact: +91 20-27411240, +91 20-27412576

**MaNaN Ashram:**
Survey No. 43, Sanas Nagar, Nandoshi Gaon, Kirkatwadi Phata, Off Sinhagad Road, Taluka Haveli, Pune district - 411024, INDIA. Contact: +91 992100 8060.

### WORLD PEACE PRAYER

*Divine Light of Love, Bliss, and Peace is Showering;*

*The Golden Light of Higher Consciousness is Rising;*

*All negativity on Earth is Dissolving;*

*Everyone is in Peace and Blissfully Shining;*

*O God, Gratitude for Everything!*

Members of Tej Gyan Foundation have been offering this impersonal mass prayer for many years. Those who are happy can offer this prayer. Those feeling low or suffering from illness can receive healing with this prayer.

If you are feeling troubled or sick, please sit to receive the healing effect of this prayer. Visualize that the divine white healing light is being showered on earth through the prayers of thousands and is also reaching you, bringing you peace and good health. You can dwell in this feeling for some time and then offer your gratitude to those offering the prayer.

### A Humble Appeal

More than a million peace lovers pray for World Peace and Global Healing every morning and evening at 9:09. Also, a prayer (in Hindi) to elevate consciousness is webcast every day on YouTube at 3:30 pm and 9:00 pm IST. Please participate in this noble endeavor.

www.ingramcontent.com/pod-product-compliance
Lightning Source LLC
LaVergne TN
LVHW041843070526
838199LV00045BA/1421